eim...

george f. palmer

1st WORLD
PUBLISHING

eim...

george f. palmer

Copyright © george f. palmer 2011

Published by 1st World Publishing
P.O. Box 2211, Fairfield, Iowa 52556
tel: 641-209-5000 • fax: 866-440-5234
web: www.1stworldpublishing.com

First Edition

LCCN: 2011943599
SoftCover ISBN: 978-1-4218-8635-0
HardCover ISBN: 978-1-4218-8638-1

dedication

i would like to dedicate this book to my wife, ellen, without whom so many stories included in this book could never have occurred. we loved and laughed and our madnesses ran together in an unending enjoyment of life. even the bad times. the love and laughter were augmented by an abiding sense of "...i got your back, and i know that you got mine".

trust. trust and the ability to forgive. that is what makes our clock tick.

i would also like to thank and acknowledge susan blaufarb not only for her services as an amanuensis, but for being a friend, advisor and fellow nut. forosoco forever.

i would like to thank the first ellen first, who, together with my dad, gave me an abiding love for words.

least but not last, i'd like to thank my best man, edward, for always being supportive, compelling and the funniest guy i ever met. nccc forever.

table of contents

lemee smell your fingers

eim sitting in a chair of the emergency room of a large long island hospital. there is an elderly homeless woman sitting next to me. she smells of urine, yeast and perspiration. quite the bouquet. i have come to the hospital at my wife's insistence to seek treatment for this stubborn flu i have seem to have contracted and am having difficulty shaking. the woman sitting next to me is exacerbating my condition exponentially. my head is swimming. i have been for a useless cat scan and am now sitting in this e.r. chair with my coat on ready to go home. my car keys are in my hand. i am expecting the doctor to tell me that i have the flu and should check back with him in a few days. i felt like shit and i wanted to go home. abruptly, my wife and a different doctor appeared at my side. this doctor told me to take my coat off because i was not leaving. he told me that my cat scan revealed that i had suffered a massive stroke and that he was taking me up to the operating room for emergency brain surgery. he told me that he was going to drill two small holes in my skull and then insert his fingers and "….milk my ventricles". milk my ventricles?? what the fuck…

as i was leaving my job on the saturday after thanksgiving in 2007, i felt what i can only describe as a starburst somewhere deep in my noodle. despite a gathering migraine and some difficulty driving, i was able to drive home. i was beginning to really not feel well and the mother of all headaches was upon me. i went to bed hoping to sweat it out. during saturday night i began vomiting and the headache was much worse. i was having trouble with my vision yet i remained convinced that i only had the flu. my wife, (a nurse), was not so certain. all day sunday my condition deteriorated until sunday night when she insisted that i visit the emergency room.

when we arrived at the hospital, blood and urine were collected and i was sent for a cat scan of my head. after that, i sat back down in the waiting room. i put my coat on and took out my car keys. i was ready to go home. a new doctor suddenly appeared with my wife and told me that i was not going home. he told me that my cat scan revealed that i had suffered a massive stroke. he further told me that it was necessary that he take me up to the operating room where he was going to drill two small holes in my head. at that point, he said, he was going to stick two of his fingers into my brain and, "… milk my ventricles". milk my ventricles ??? …

i put my car keys in my pocket and took my coat off. soon i was in a hospital gown lying on a gurney being whisked upstairs with the neuro-surgeon. he kept saying things like, "… stay with me, george" and "how many fingers am i holding up, george". stuff like that. in the elevator, on the way to the operating room, i asked him, "are you really going to "milk my ventricles?". he brought his face close to mine, looked me deep in the eye, and said, "…yes. i am". next thin i knew, i was being transferred from the gurney onto the operating table. it was so cold. a gas mask dropped out of the ceiling and was placed over my mouth and face. i breathed deeply and drifted off…

and then i woke up. rudely. i was choking and sputtering for i was still being extubated. immediately, the surgeon was in my face checking me out. " george! george! look at me! follow my finger… follow my finger… good. o.k., now reach out and touch your finger to your nose. good. very good. how do you feel?" i was still groggy. his face was mere inches from mine as he studied me. i made eye contact with him and said, "did you milk my ventricles?". he moved in even closer and said, "yes. i did." i stared into his eyes for a second and said, "lemee smell your fingers." he held my gaze for a moment and then abruptly left. he returned a minute later with my wife in tow. he asked, "is this his normal affect? is he alright?" my wife leaned into me and looked deep into my eyes. "are you o.k.?" it was so good to see her. i squeezed her fingers and nodded my head as a tear began to well up. she turned to the surgeon and said, " he's okay". and i was.

let them catch us

eim flying through the air because i have chosen to ride my bike down a steep hill at caumsett state park. the pitch of the slope and the bumpy terrain have conspired to eject me and cause me grievous consternation as i realize that i am in for a rough landing...

it is a beautiful early summer's morn. because it is a monday, i'm off from my job. as i stare out the kitchen window at the magnificence of the day, a smile grows large on my face as i espy my 12 year old son, michael, happily walking up the drive. i had forgotten that he would be home early due to the fact that it was exam week at school.

when he got in, i asked him if he felt like going for a bike ride to caumsett state park, an undeveloped state park on the long island sound, just north of huntington, ny. the hills there are great. i recalled the good times i had had there, riding my bike over the pitted lanes and down the grassy hills. mike said "sounds good". we loaded up the bikes into our '94 dodge caravan and headed out to caumsett.

somewhere along the way mike asked if we could stop at a deli so that he could get roast beef on a roll with lettuce, mayo, salt and pepper. i said i knew of such a place in cold spring harbor. we stopped and mike got his sandwich. i got the same sandwich mike got. we also bought a large bag of potato chips, ½ pound of german potato salad, a quart of milk, a peach snapple and two pieces of chocolate cake, so the paper bag they put the lunches in was filled to the brim.

we arrived at caumsett, got the bikes out and started riding down the pitted path. my main objective was a large building by the water that queens college was using as a campus extension. behind the building was a large grassy hill that rolled gently down to a beautiful fresh water pond. beyond that, bluffs overlooked the long island sound.

as we rode down the bike path, we came up behind a couple who were walking down the bike path holding hands. there were shrubs and bushes alongside the bike path which made it impossible for mike and i to pass them.

"beep-beep" i said in what i thought was a friendly tone of voice. no response. "beep-beep" again, this time distinctly louder. the couple stopped holding hands and separated to let us through. as we rode through i thought i detected annoyed scowls. i figured that no matter how annoyed they were it could never diminish the "high" mike and i were enjoying on that fine summer day.

we rode on until we at last came to the queens college extension. we got off our bikes and walked them around back to the hill that i was looking for. but things had changed. the hill was there alright, but it had become quite a bit steeper and there were now two large signs which warned, **"no bike riding"**. mike and i stood astride our bikes on the crest of the hill looking down. mike turned to me and said, "what should we do?" i shifted the large paper bag with our lunches in it from my right arm to my left arm, gave him a wink, said "let them catch us!!" and shoved off down the hill.

immediately i realized that i had made a mistake. with only my right hand on the handle bar and my left arm holding the lunches, i had very little control of my bike as it hurtled down the hill. a further challenge to me became apparent when i squeezed the right handbrake and nothing, and i mean **nothing**, happened. pieces of bike began to fly off. a reflector here, a kick stand there. i heard michael compassionately screaming with glee behind me. out flew the sandwiches from the bag. out flew the milk and potato chips. then out flew me! up in the air, ass over tea kettle. the bike went left, i went right, and came down hard (right in the middle of a poison ivy patch, i found out a few days later).

i think i was in shock a bit, and as i slowly realized that i was neither dead nor paralyzed, i became aware of maniacal cackling off to my right. i turned to face my dear son michael who was in the throes of unabated hilarity. tears were rolling down his cheeks.

"that's the funniest thing i ever saw", he commented compassionately. "pieces of your bike kept flying off. and then you went flying too! ha! ha! ha! ha! ha! ha!... ooooo! ha! ha! ha! ha! ha! ha!"

now, i love my son, truly i do. but the image of him **enjoying** my misfortune so very thoroughly was, in my opinion, bad form. as i tried to stand, i felt much pain in my tailbone. much pain. as i wiped dirt and grass from my arms and legs, i looked first back up the hill at the trail of broken bike bits and deli delights, and then down to where my treacherous bike lay looking more like a calder sculpture than a bicycle. the seat was facing backward, the handlebars were askew and the front wheel had collapsed into a distinct "v" shape.

i slowly regrouped and set myself to the task of bending the "v" out of my front tire. having no tools, i attempted to straighten out the tire the way people used to do it in the old days... by jumping on it! so i jumped. the first two jumps straightened out the tire some. i figured one... more... jump ought to do it. yup. i positioned the tire and then jumped up into the air with both feet. unfortunately, when my feet landed on the wheel, the wheel spun, causing me to take yet another embarrassing tumble.

as i got to my hands and knees, i again heard laughter off to my right. i knew it wasn't my son. he was in my line of vision and knew by the shade of purple my face had turned that laughing was a bad idea. i turned my head a little more

george f. palmer

and saw the two handholding lovers from the bike path. they were laughing. they were pointing. i was fuming. i was glaring. and then the girl took a step toward us and yelled out "beep-beep". egad. hoisted on my own petard.

blind wrestler

eim in the old gym at north country community college, in saranac lake ny. the saints wrestling team (of which i am a member) is about to begin its match against the suny potsdam (or was it plattsburgh?), j.v. wrestling team. across the mat from us, their team sits in folding chairs eyeballing and sizing us up. we are doing the same thing to them. as i measure up their wrestlers to determine who their 142 pounder is, i see a wrestler of frightening countenance on their bench. he is a very muscular black man and he is obviously very blind. his head lolls about on his stumpy neck in a stevie wonder kind of way. but it is his eyes that draw you in. because they are rolled up in his head, you can only see the whites of them. however, you can tell by the blood vessels that they are moving. the whites of his eyes juxtaposed against that oilskin epidermis made him appear slightly crazy. sitting next to him was the fellow i determined was their 142 pounder, a tall, wiry guy i thought i would be able to muscle.

as the matches wore on, i was surprised to see the tall, wiry guy come out and wrestle our 136 pounder. it slowly dawned on me that i would probably be wrestling the blind, crazy-looking guy. sure enough, when i got up to stand on my side of the circle, i watched as two of my opponent's team mates escorted this nightmare to his position opposite me. immediately, i was drawn to those vacant, searching eyes. the ref explained to me that because of his handicap, we would start the match off with our arms outstretched and our fingers touching. this closer proximity gave his countenance an even

george f. palmer

more intimidating demeanor.

at the whistle he somehow clamped onto my forearms and then, like a sewing machine, he stitched me right up my body. wham! wham! wham! i was completely overwhelmed. i don't think the match was 60 seconds old when i found myself on the wrong side of a cradle listening to the horrible acoustic sound of the refs hand slapping the foam mat. as the ref lifted my opponents hand up in victory, i realized that i had not even broken a sweat. very, very embarrassing.

septic soup and sesames

eim north of moosehead lake, maine, driving a 28' rented r.v. my girlfriend (ellen and i were sparking by then) and our two dogs were taking a prolonged vacation through new england. it was a great trip. many laughs and many adventures. the r.v. was outstanding and commodious.

the septic system in the r.v. required us to connect up to a pumping station in order to empty the system. the pumping stations were few and far between in rural northern maine, however, and one day the need too empty the septic system became malodorously clear. the trip to the nearest pumping station was almost two hours away. i decided that drastic times called for drastic measures. i explained my plan to ellen. we would find a suitable dirt road in the middle of nowhere and i would unscrew the cap of the septic system and simply have the effluence let fly right there on the road. i know, i know, it's disgusting. i figured that it would rain soon and all my sins would be washed away so to speak. i'm not proud of it, but i did do it, so what the hell and (with all due respect), fuck you, too.

at any rate, we found a suitable dirt road and i drove down it for about 2 miles. i stopped the r.v. in the middle of the road, left the engine running, and walked back to unscrew the cap to the septic system. as i squatted down, i slowly began to unscrew the cap all the while thinking of the best way to avoid the flood that would inevitably splash out. righty tighty, lefty loosey, right? slowly i turned the cap to the left and then… bang! the cap exploded out of my hand, banged off my head (knocking off my yankee's cap), and dropped into the disgusting soup that was now issuing forth with such foul gusto. i squeamishly reached into the soup, grabbed the cap and sprinted into the r.v. as i put it in gear and drove away, i became aware of my girl's uproarious laughter. she was pointing at my head. in between cackles, she blurted out "….there are all sesame seeds in your hair". and indeed there were. the pressure of the accumulated methane gas conspired with the residue of a recent trip to macdonald's to elicit such joy from my better half. ain't love grand?.

cry baby cry

eim hunkered down in the privet hedge of my neighbors, the moores, who lived across the street. i am hiding. i am crying. i am six. and i don't wanna go to school. it is perhaps 20 minutes after 9:00 a.m., the time 1st grade commenced. my mother had walked me down to newbridge road school (now the heritage arms apartment complex) and dropped me off on line at about 8:55. it had been no mean feat. it was the second day of 1st grade and i had a case of terminal separation anxiety. on the first day of 1st grade, i had sat down in my seat more miserable than any child should ever be. from the moment i sat down, i sobbed uncontrollably. i was a mess. i couldn't stop. the teacher, mrs. gordon tried to calm me down as best she could but to no avail. when she asked me what was wrong i could only wail, "…i'm h-o-o-omesick…" mrs. gordon had had to walk over to the intercom and ask the secretary to call my mother to come and get me. all the other kids kept staring at me as i wept and blubbered. it was a bizarre scene as mrs. gordon actually began trying to teach despite my unnerving ululations. an embarrassing 15 minutes passed until my mom appeared at the door to take me home. as i got up from my seat, i felt a score of eyes burning into my back. as i walked out the door into the september sunlight, i remember feeling ashamed and acknowledged to myself that i had not passed muster. my mother was concerned as we walked home. our conversation (her monologue) was half consolation and half scolding. as i watched t.v. that surreal morning i had one of my first experiences of guilt. my mother hugged and kissed

george f. palmer

me and told me that things would go better the next day at school. i did not sleep well that night and in the morning all the anxiety and apprehension washed over me again. i told my mother that i didn't want to go to school. i cried again. my mother tried to reassure me as she dressed me, but i remained inconsolable. i cried most of the way to school imploring my mother, "please ... don't make me go to school..."

as we got to the back of the school where the 1st graders lined up, my mother leaned over and kissed me, telling me everything was going to be alright. and then, with some trepidation i'm sure, she turned and walked away. i was alone, on line with those kids! other kids on the line were talking to each other, or looking at baseball cards with one another. i never felt more alone.

the classroom door opened and my classmates began to file in. panic swept over me and i left the line and bolted. i ran down newbridge road and made a left onto lawn drive. i was walking and crying, so very lost, and i remember the sunlight feeling strangely cold. if you made a right at the end of lawn drive, you would be on cypress avenue where we lived. if you made a left onto dogwood avenue, you could still access our house via balsam avenue and argyle road. i made a left.

i had never been on my own in the neighborhood and despite the beauty of the autumn day the houses of my neighborhood looked strangely sinister and foreboding. i walked down to the end of balsam avenue to argyle road. from that vantage point i could see my house, my home, where i desperately wished to be but i knew that i could not go. what a conundrum for a 6 year old! i stood on the corner staring at my house fretting, rocking back and forth, and trying to develop a plan of action for myself. none was forthcoming. i began to cry again and i realized that if i stood there any longer one of my neighbors might see me and notify my mother or, worse yet, call the police.

i walked down argyle road toward my house, vigilant eyes

glued on our kitchen window for any sign of my mom. the moore family home on argyle road was bordered by a 3 foot high privet hedge and it was behind this hedge i slipped to begin a surveillance of my house and form some kind of plan. i crawled under the hedge and lay there in the dirt in my school clothes, eyes pinned on my house across the street.

as the minutes passed, i became acutely aware of my micro-environment. there was an earthworm digging in the topsoil less than a foot from my face. i enjoyed watching it because it momentarily distracted me from my plight. there was still dew on the clover in moore's yard and i watched it glisten and shine. i watched a sprinkler go on at the luvitch house and an oil truck stop to make a delivery at the carbonaro's.

as i stared at my house, i watched as the front door opened and my mother emerged. she walked down the walk looking first right, then left. i knew in my heart she was looking for me. she walked onto the sidewalk, one hand on her hip and the other one shielding her eyes from the sun as she peered up and down the block. i wanted to scream out "mom!", but i was way too ashamed and afraid.

my mother walked around the house and then back into the front yard where she cupped her hand and yelled my name out loud. i could hear fear in her voice as she yelled up the block, then back down the block. i think that the fear in my mom's voice was the thing that got to me. i slowly stood up and raised my hand to indicate to her where i was. my bottom lip was trembling terribly and i could not speak. i walked through the hedge and stood on the curb across the street from my house watching as my mother crossed cypress ave. and strode towards me, an emotional glass of water to an emotionally thirsty boy. i was crying as i looked into her face trying hard to gauge her temperament. she put her arms around me and then right there on the curb, rocked me back and forth in the sweetest, tightest, most consoling hug any kid anywhere ever got. cars passed and i saw them staring at us, but neither one of us cared. when she had hugged and rocked enough tears out

of me, she pulled back and looked deeply into my eyes. i saw
(and not for the last time) a look of worry come over her. she
bundled me up in her arms and carried me across the street to
where i needed to be then….home.

peeping into hell

eim 15 and standing on my tiptoes looking over the car-bonaro's 6' stockade fence into the williams' yard where a policeman's grappling hook has snared the lifeless, effluence covered body of my 8 year old neighbor, peter williams, from the collapsed cesspool in his front yard...

perhaps 3 hours prior to the the cop cars and fire engines pulling up in front of the williams' house, young peter had ridden up to our front door selling cub scout cookies. i remember that he was a stutterer, but a real nice kid. "w-w-wanna b-b-buy some c-c-cookies, george?"

my friend skip and i were returning from archie's lunch-eonette, on newbridge road, where we had enjoyed cherry cokes served up by surly old lee jahrsdoerffer. as we rode our bikes back down cypress avenue, we noticed emergency vehicles pulling up at the williams house next door to skip's. we ditched our bikes in skip's driveway and made our way through the maze that was the carbonaro garden to the gray-brown 6' stockade fence that separated the williams' yard and the carbonaro yard. we stepped up onto the fence and peered over.

we saw about five cops holding up some blankets to sepa-rate the neighborhood rubberneckers that had gathered on the sidewalk from the cop who had the grappling hook. there was a gaping hole on the front lawn, approximately 6' – 7' in diam-eter. across that hole the police had laid some boards. on those boards one cop knelt on all fours dropping and re-dropping a grappling hook into the fetid depths. skip and i had outflanked the police and the crowd, and from our vantage point, we had a perfect, horrible view of what transpired next.

directly in front of us was the cop with the grappling hook. to our left was the line of cops and the crowd. to our right, in the front doorway of her home, was mrs. williams. she was holding the screen door open with her right foot. in her right hand she held the receiver of a telephone. she was talking animatedly into it as she surveyed the desperate activity occurring out on her front lawn.

suddenly, the cop with the grappling hook jerked his head to the side and in a voice fraught with horror and realization, blurted out, "sarge! …" the rope attached to the grappling hook had been slack as the cop had trolled back and forth, and now i noticed the rope was taut as if there were a heavy weight attached to it at the other end.

"no-o-o-o-o…!" screamed mrs. williams at the exact same moment. the scream was unlike any i had ever heard. it was a terrible, primal scream. gutteral. horrible. i turned my head to see her. she had dropped the phone. as she screamed, she was making spasmodic chopping motions in the air with her hands. her eyes were bugged out. the emotion coming out of her scared the hell out of me. i turned my eyes back to the cop with the grappling hook. he and a couple of other cops were pulling hard on the rope and then suddenly the corpse of beautiful young peter williams broke the surface. one of the cops wretched and puked, and then he started sobbing in a weird way, too.

as i watched peter's head and shoulders break the surface, all covered with wet toilet paper and sewage, it became too much for me. a little sensory overload. i dropped down into a squatting position and looked up at skip who was still peering over the stockade fence. i could still hear mrs. williams screaming faintly from deep in her house as i watched the front lawn action reflected on skippy's face. it took a long time to fall asleep that night.

gan aft agley

eim standing in the cold adirondack rain with my arms wrapped around a pine tree and my pants around my ankles as i shoot corn laden diarrhea into the upper, middle and lower branches of another pine tree that is perhaps 3 feet behind me.

i'm afraid that when my wife and i were courting i was a bit of a bully when it came to choosing summer vacation destinations. this particular year, i wanted to go camping in the adirondacks and somehow bulldozed (saint) ellen into agreeing. all this despite the stubborn facts that we had very little capital, the only vehicle between us that was up to the trip was her 1971 yellow vw bug, and wherever we went we would have to bring spot and amos, my, not her, dogs.

it was the second week of september. the leaves in the adirondacks had begun to change. we got off the northway at exit 30 and traveled west to lake placid where we spent the first night in a motel. ellen's volkswagen looked a bit like the truck that made the journey to california in <u>the grapes of wrath</u> with henry fonda. ellen said it looked like the truck in <u>the beverly hillbillies</u>. both observations were correct. our entire luggage (and i use the word luggage very, very loosely) was tied atop the bug, crowned by an acoustic guitar of mine, which sat regally atop our luggage unencumbered, unfettered and uncased. i remember thinking, as we drove through a thunderstorm, that the exposure my guitar was undergoing was probably going to have a deleterious effect on it. little did i know then that that particular thought was about to pale when compared to the events which were to transpire.

george f. palmer

our second day was spent exploring first saranac, and then tupper lakes. it rained most of the day and so we grabbed a motel room for the night and promised ourselves that come hell or high water (both of which were to show up), that we would use our wonderful camping gear and camp out on beautiful lake eaton. yesirree…

we drove around the misty adirondacks for most of the next day. we stopped at a roadside vegetable stand where we bought some sweet corn for the feast we were going to prepare that night at lake eaton public campground. we had steaks, burgers, salads, kebobs, chicken, corn, tab and beer. perfect.

because of the great distances between places in the adirondacks, i miscalculated our e.t.a. at lake eaton and by the time we arrived, signed in, and got to our campsite, the sun had set and a cold steady mist hung rudely in the air. we began to unload the car. i had a beautiful, 3 burner coleman stove that my sister had returned to me just prior to our departure from long island. it was my pride and joy. our tent was state of the art and commodious – 12' x 15' with 2 rooms and 3 windows. ellen's brother had borrowed it earlier in the summer and told us how great it was.

as we unpacked, we gave the dogs some well deserved free reign. i watched as they gamboled along the lakeshore and the darkening woods surrounding our campsite. this came to an abrupt halt when an angry male voice boomed out from our neighboring campsite. "hey! get outta here… hey… get these dogs outta here!!". "sorry", i said. "…spot! amos! get back over here! sorry!" the dogs, the wet, wet dogs, came back and i admonished them and told them to stick around. they looked at me as if they understood (yeah, right) i figured "well, **that's** taken care of"!

i carried the box with the tent in it over to the wet picnic table. i figured it would take 20 minutes to assemble the tent. half-hour tops. as i spilled the contents of the box onto the table, i realized that something was missing. oh. my. god… the poles! the tent poles were not there! ellen's brother must have forgotten to pack them up after he had borrowed it! bastard! i ran back to the car to see if the poles had somehow fallen out in there. as i fumbled in the trunk, i heard another roar from my neighbor's campsite. "…get these dogs outta here!". "sorry. sorry 'bout that! here boys!. spot… amos… c'mon!"

the dogs were now thoroughly soaked and filthy with mud. i took some rope and tied them to a tree. that oughta hold them? there. now what to do? yes, but first things first. i walked over to the large cooler which was filled with ice and beer. i reached in, pulled out the first (but not the last), cold budweiser and sat down to cogitate. as i sat there in the rain cogitating and power slamming that first beer, the dogs began to bark. alot. i just looked at them. then i looked at my ellen and she did not look happy. i pulled the cooler closer to me and began to cogitate harder. about 3 budweisers worth of cogitation later, a plan slowly began to form in my fuzzy head.

there was a large tree in our campsite that sported an over-hanging branch, perhaps 12' – 13' feet from the ground. i reckoned that if i could just… somehow… shimmy… up… that tree with a rope, i could somehow fasten… the rope… to the top of the tent and then somehow… perhaps… hoist the tent like a flag and give us a smaller, yet viable, living quarters. a little dutch courage in the form of two more budweisers and up the tree i began to shimmy. well, perhaps shimmy is not the correct term to describe my climbing technique.

i had put a rope through two loops at the top of the tent. i took the rope and sort of jumped/hugged this huge tree. as i shimmied, i realized that it must appear i am humping the tree in some sort of biocenotic porno movie. the skin on my inner arms and legs began to abrade against the rough bark. up, up the tree i clambered until i reached the branch to which i wished to tie the tent. i pulled the rope and hoisted the tent up until it reached the branch. i tied the rope around the branch and… voila! it worked!

sort of. the problem was, that the original 12' x 15' area of the tent was now reduced to an area of approximately 4 square feet. in addition, the floor of the tent was not lying flat on the ground. it rose up in one corner and sloped down to the other, further reducing our area of floor space. ellen put our two sleeping bags in the tent and there was just enough room for them. the sagging of the tent, coupled with the misty air made for an uncomfortable feeling of claustrophobia when you were inside it. ellen was not impressed with my improvisation, and was not of the opinion that we would last the night. i pooh-poohed her negativity, threw back another beer and set off to begin the al fresco banquet i had been envisioning in my mind since we arrived.

and to cook this feast, i had brought along my favorite piece of camping equipment: a 3 burner coleman stove. 3 burners! i could cook everything at once! i took the stove from the canvas bag it was in, filled the tank with coleman fuel and began to pump air into the tank to bring up the gas. but something was wrong. the leather compression gasket on the pump was ripped in half. it rendered the stove useless. my sister must have forgotten to tell me it was broken after she had borrowed it! bastard!

what to do? as i began cogitating again and snapping open yet another beer, the dogs started barking again. alot. i just stared at them, all the while slowly spinning the useless compression gasket between my thumb and index fingers. my eyes glazed over. somewhere in the distance someone was yelling to "shut those dogs up! it's 9:30 at night!" i realized that i was mumbling to myself as i sat there in the rain in the dark. now, behind me, from the tent, came the sound of weeping. several mosquitoes circled my head but i did not even attempt to shoo them away. my reverie was broken by the insistent hollering of my neighbor who again yelled out, "…shut those dogs up!".

i snapped, stood up, and yelled back, "yeah, yeah, yeah. fuck you, too" with beer enhanced conviction and gusto. the weeping in the tent grew louder. i walked over to the wet filthy dogs, untied them, and led them into the collapsing tent and drunkenly explained to my poor sobbing girlfriend, that the guy at the next campsite was "being an asshole"…, i gotta put the dogs in here!... (hic)!". as i exited the tent i noticed the angle of the tent had resulted in perhaps an inch or two of rain water accumulating in the low corner. that can't be good. i walked back into the rainy night and realized that i had to pee. into the woods i walked, dropped trou, and stood there with my hands on my hips, head tilted back, and peed into the cold, wet adirondack air. aahhhh…

as i stood there peeing i suddenly realized that all was not lost. oh, sweet afflatus! why, if i could just find some dry wood, i could use the coleman fuel to start a great fire that would provide light, warmth, cheer and a source of heat for cooking steaks, chicken, kebobs and corn. perfect!!! i walked a bit deeper into the woods and started collecting wet logs and branches. it was of course, no problem finding wet logs and branches in the rain, and i had soon collected a large amount of them. however, on my last trip out of the woods with the soggy firewood, i stumbled in the mud and managed to open up a 3" gash on my right shin. not to worry. nothing a few bellowed expletives couldn't fix.

i piled the soggy logs and faggots on the stone circle which served as a campfire/cooking pit, and reached for the old reliable - coleman fuel. i poured what i considered to be a fair amount of fuel on the wood, stepped back and lit a wood match, which i threw on top of the pile. there was a brief flash of flame, and then the fire quickly fizzled out due to the wet wood and the rain, which, by the way, had increased in intensity.

i picked up the coleman fuel again, unscrewed the cap, and held the can upside down over the wet wood. glunk - glunk, glunk – glunk, glunk – glunk, out poured the fuel. "that oughta do it…", thought i. i lit a second match and immediately wished i had not. a flash of fire exploded sending flames 20' into the air, knocking me down and singeing the hair on my arms, legs and head. not only that, but i had somehow set the low, wet branches of the tree my tent was tied to, on fire.

i stood up and looked around for something to throw at the flaming tree to knock the fire down. the first thing i saw were some of the ears of corn from our erstwhile dinner in a cardboard box. i reached in, grabbed a few ears and began throwing them up into the blazing branches which burned in the rain. somehow, between my corn throws and the natural action of rain on fire, the branches were quickly extinguished. i remember sitting on the picnic table in the rain, heart pounding and enjoying the wonderful odor of my own burnt, wet hair. i looked down at the ground and noticed that the steak i had intended to broil was lying face down in the mud and wet pine needles. i must have knocked it off the table in my mad dash to get the corn. wonderful. beautiful.

i turned my head and looked at the "fire" which was throwing forth a spastic lick of flame every now and then, but was mostly just smoking. i threw some wet charcoal on the smoldering pit and sat down to cogitate again. as i sat there drinking, i mean cogitating, i thought to myself that i'm just going to boil a pot of water, cook the remaining ears of corn, chow down and go to bed.

i got a cooking pot and walked down the muddy path to beautiful lake eaton. i scooped up a pot full of it and splashed my way back to the campsite. i set the pot on the "fire" and sat down to learn and appreciate the wisdom of the old maxim that "... a watched pot never boils".

as i sat there besotted and wet, gazing at the pot of water, i began to nod off. my chin would drop... drop....drop slowly onto my chest and then my head would snap back up with a start again. i looked at the water in the pot. it was not boiling. slowly my eyes would close and again my chin would slowly drop to my chest. this happened perhaps a half dozen times. the next time it happened i'm pretty sure i saw thin streams of steam emanating from the water. "close enough!", i thought to myself. i dumped four ears of corn into the "boiling" water and sat back to await this decidedly scaled down version of my envisioned feast.

i immediately nodded off and when i awoke a few minutes later, the corn was still sitting there in the warmish water, not cooking. "done!" i thought to myself. i poured the lake water (well, most of it) from the pot and proceeded to lather those ears of corn up with butter. i sat down in the rain and ate those four ears of corn and when i was done i stood up, walked over to the tent, farted loudly, and dragged my greasy-faced self into the tent where i lay down and fell asleep snoring loudly next to my lucky girlfriend.

sometime around 4:00 a.m., i bolted upright in my sleeping bag. my bowels were twisting and writhing as if there were a living creature inside me. the contractions and spasms were of such intensity that tears formed in my eyes. i quickly realized that an unfortunate explosion was imminent and i jumped up and staggered to the tent door which had been zippered shut by a zipper i could not now locate. i stood there following the zipper tracks with my fingers like a blind man, all the while squeezing my cheeks together, bending and stooping in a feverish watusi. i finally found the zipper, opened the screen door and stumbled back out into the dark, wet, adirondack night. i knew that off to my right perhaps 50 yards away was a bathroom, but in my present state there was no way i could go that far and remain tidy.

i stumbled into the woods perhaps 10 yards from the tent, dropped trou and let fly. the first blast knocked me forward into a pine tree which i immediately hugged. i stood there bent over hugging that tree with my pants around my ankles and my sigmoid performing dance routines that god never intended my sigmoid to perform.

there was a soft light coming through the woods from the 50 watt bulb which served to illuminate the bathrooms. as i turned my head slowly around i saw first, that a large sea of mosquitoes were swarming round my besieged buttocks, and second, how high up my corn-laden stool had shot into the upper branches of another pine tree which was perhaps 3 feet behind me. how did i do that? that's over my head! wow! i endured explosive spasm after explosive spasm. my psychotic anus had taken on a mind of its own as it sprayed diarrhea and shot corn first this way, then that way. no tree was safe.

after 20 minutes or so, the convulsions abated. either that, or i was out of ammo. as i pulled my pants up, i realized that my legs and butt were covered in hundreds of mosquito bites. i slowly turned round and saw the pine tree which had caught the brunt of my anal antics. it looked beautiful! in the soft, wet light the corn looked like christmas ornaments and the diarrhea like wet brown tinsel! ho! ho! ho!

i stumbled back to the tent, threw open the flap, stuck my head in and said to ellen, "we're leaving. now!"

"now?"

"now!"

"what about all our stuff?"

"leave it!"

we took our clothes from the tent and left all the food and camping equipment where it was. as we walked up the path toward the parking lot, i spied... oh no! it can't be... but yes. there it was, right there on the path... my christmas tree! when i ran into the woods i must have cut right through to the path. my god, it was ugly! we walked past it and on up to the parking lot. we threw our clothes into the trunk, our two muddied and panting dogs into the back seat, ourselves in the front seats of the bug and sat sullenly in the dark for a moment.

i gathered my wits (?). i turned the ignition key, pushed the clutch down, put the car into 1st gear, pressed down on the gas pedal and heard an ominous "ching" as the accelerator cable snapped and the gas pedal fell useless, to the floor.

i began to shake and quake. steam emerged from both ears. i gripped the steering wheel so violently i thought i might pulverize it. ellen examined my mug with curiosity. i took a deep breath, relaxed my grip on the steering wheel, and got out of the car.

volkswagens had a very accessible spring loaded throttle on the engine back then. i figured that if i could find a stick or piece of wood i would be able to wedge it into the throttle, thus giving me enough gas to accelerate through the gears. i found a small pine cone and wedged into the throttle, which loudly opened it up all the way. i jumped back into the car, put the car into first, clutched, and shot out of that parking lot at about 50 miles per hour. our heads snapped back. the two dogs went tumbling up into the rear window. gravel spewed from under our wheels. i shot quickly through the gears until we got to the main road which led into the village of long lake where we were able to procure a motel room for the night. it was the last time ellen and i ever went camping.

ugly moondance soccer

eim staring out at the dance floor at aspens, in wantagh, ny, as dancers kick around my front tooth cap that i have accidentally spit from my mouth as i sang "moondance", by van morrison.

i had one of my front teeth kicked out by a football teammate back in the sixties. the dentist put a post in and placed a cap over it. shortly after high school i snapped the post. i had it fixed and re-snapped it several times after that. i found that i could avoid the costly and time consuming trips to the dentist if i crazy glued the tooth into my mouth. brilliant! the glue never lasted more than a day or so, so i was constantly re-gluing the cap. this was not without its pitfalls as often i would annoyingly end up gluing the fast bonding crazy glue to the cap, or to my finger or lip. many was the night i would be singing with the top layer of skin from my index finger bonded to my front tooth in an obvious fingerprint.

anyway, sometime during my second set, while i was singing "moondance", i hit a high note and out shot (and i mean shot) my front tooth. i watched in horror as it hit some guy in the shoulder and fell to the dance floor among the shuffling feet.

i was mortified. i mumbled "short-break…" into the microphone, put down my guitar, and waded out onto the dance floor. my eyes were glued (sorry, no pun intended) downward as i moved among the dancers, embarrassed and hoping beyond hope that the cap would come into view.

and then i saw it next to the base of one of the tables. i casually sauntered over and bent down as if to tie my sneaker. i grabbed the cap. i was so happy. next, i had to hop into my car and drive to 7-11 to buy a quick tube of crazy glue. i got the glue, got the tooth back in, and got back on stage all within 20 minutes. i wasn't even late starting the second set!

george f. palmer

dad vs the beatles

eim lying on the aqua marine rug (no foam matting underneath) in the living room of our house on cypress avenue watching the beatles on the ed sullivan show. it is 1964.

for weeks, my sister linda had been raving about this band from england called the beatles. i took my sister's appraisal very seriously. she was the one who had interested me in music. she was a fan of lesley gore, the shirelles and bands like that. i grew up listening to "judy's turn to cry", "it's my party", "he's a rebel", "the doo ron ron" song (?). i had no brothers so i didn't know from elvis or buddy holly. the first 45 i purchased (for 79¢) at models east meadow was "my boyfriend's back" by the angels. i was eleven and i wrote in black magic marker, "property of george palmer...you touch, you die!", across the front of the record. i guess i was over reacting and paranoid even then.

when 8:00 came that sunday night, everyone in the family including my mother and father were in the living room tuned in to cbs ny, channel 2. eventually, ed got round to introducing the boys who performed and transformed me and a whole lot of other people. my sister linda and i were thrilled. my other three sisters demonstrated a modicum of interest while my parents offered up a combination of concern and ennui. the evening passed and life went on.

twenty years later i was talking to my dad who was in a nursing home due to the aftermath of a terrible stroke. the conversation shifted to that february night in 1964. he said that he remembered it, too. he said that he watched me become transfixed. it made him sad. he told me that as he watched me watching them, he realized that he had lost me forever. i was twelve years old.

he who laughs wet laughs wettest

eim in our new house on pilgrim lane, westbury. nanny (anne), my mother-in-law, ellen and myself are investigating the wonders of the ultra-modern (to us) mechanisms of our new kitchen faucet. at our previous home, in east meadow, the kitchen faucet had a left handle for hot water and a right handle for cold water. to create warm water you would mix hot and cold, left and right. our new kitchen faucet had a bizarre design. the faucet itself resembled a scaled down version of one of the alien spaceships in "war of the worlds". it had an armature hanging off the right side which could be manipulated by pushing it up, down, left, and right. this was, alternatively, hot, cold, fast and slow. there was also a red dot ¼ of the way up the shaft of the faucet and, just behind that, a seam.

as we three stood there with the (hot) water running, nanny pressed the red dot and the faucet folded in two causing a very startling spray of quite warm water to spray, actually gush, from the compromised faucet. the spray/gush caught me in a ralph kramdenesque moment, with its full force catching me flush in the face and hair. shocked, i recoiled and fought to stop the deluge. after a moment, which seemed like 10 minutes, i succeeded in stemming the flow. ellen, anne and i looked at each other and burst out laughing.

i remember that i was angry about getting wet at first but mom, and than especially nanny, began to laugh at the situation (not me) and i could not help but laugh at the situation which was that, this time, the joke was on me and i was the guy who ended up squirting himself in the face with the proverbial seltzer bottle. we laughed for along time after that and i think the three of us were always a little closer after that. you know, warmer.

george f. palmer

the boat crash

eim standing in the stern of fred's boat and i am having a moment frozen in time as i begin to reconstruct the events that have put us in such peril…

one summer saturday we drove out to cutchogue,ny, on the north fork of long island where our newlywed friends, fred and nancy, lived. we had been there before. fred had a 23' boat and he would take us to an island in peconic bay. he said he was the only one who knew of its existence. he had a large inflated inner tube that we would sit on as he towed us around the bay. it was a lot of fun. as the sun went down, he would make a fire and we would have picnic feasts.

on this particular beautiful summer day, fred, mike and myself went on a short trip in the boat to the other side of robbin's island to try our hand at fishing. fishing was not good, and after about an hour or so, we headed back. at one point fred was letting mike drive the boat under his auspices and supervision. i was in the stern of the boat trolling as we headed home. i heard my son say, "fred… there's another boat. you'd better take it". i looked up and saw a boat about triple the size of ours bearing down on us. at this point, fred took over. the boats were about 80 – 100 yards apart at this point. i turned around and went back to trolling.

after another moment or so, i heard fred say, "…look at this asshole…" i could feel the boat zig-zagging as fred throttled forward at full steam in an effort to avoid the other boat. evidently, every time fred zigged, the guy in the bigger boat zagged, leaving us on a high speed collision course. "shit!", yelled fred. i stood up quickly and saw what appeared to be an aircraft carrier bearing down on us with grim intent. i lurched forward to grab mike (who was standing next to fred, by the wheel) and the next thing i remember was waking up on the deck of the boat and not remembering who, what, where, when or why. i was also aware that i was deaf. i stood up and felt a sharp pain on my right ankle. at about this time i began to get my hearing back because i became aware of mike crying. i saw him by the motor, in the stern of the boat, and limped over to him. as i checked him out, i became aware of smoke coming from the conked out engine and water that was coming in through a cracked seam in the fiberglass of the boat. i realized fred was gone and searched the water around the boat for him to no avail. then i saw him. he had been flung out of the boat and sprawled across the bow of the boat. he wasn't moving. i though he was dead. as i crossed back toward the front of the boat, i began screaming,"….fred! fred! ….somebody call 911!". i climbed out onto the bow of the boat to help him, and as i got close to him, i saw a jet of blood gush out of his head that shot up into the air about 3 feet. it freaked me out. i could hear mike crying as i pulled off my t-shirt and began to wrap it around fred's head as a tourniquet. and then… splurt! a geyser of blood shot straight up into my face and hair. yuck!

"help… help!…" again i screamed. i looked out at the other boats. they were in a circle around us perhaps 35 – 40 yards away. it seemed to me that no one was doing anything to help us, yet everyone was staring at us. perhaps the smoke made them afraid that we were about to blow up. anyway, at about this time, a small (14') rented rowboat appeared with a young man and young woman on board. "ahoy"…, the young man said (yes, he actually said "ahoy"). "….grab this line". he threw a long rope from his boat onto our boat which landed across fred's body. i picked it up, and slowly, they began towing us toward the new suffolk marina. when we got there, the waiting ambulances took fred and mike to eastern long island medical center and left me to fend for myself as far as locating and rescuing ellen, nancy (fred's wife), kelly and maggie.

the emt's suggested that i walk (limp) over to the new suffolk coast guard station and see if maybe they could help me. you must remember that i was shirtless, shoeless and covered in blood. my hair was matted to my head with the blood of fred. people walking along the dock at the marina stared at, and avoided, me as i limped along. when i got to the little coast guard station, i opened the door and found myself face to face with two young (they looked about 16 years old) coast guardsmen. they looked upon my bloody visage with mouths agape.

"we've been in a boat accident..." i said, "...they've taken my friend and my son to the hospital. my friend's wife and my wife and kids are stranded on an island somewhere out there in the bay. it's getting dark, and i'm sure they're wondering what has become of us."

"what's the name of the island?"

"i don't know."

well, then how are we supposed to find it?"

"i don't know?"

they looked at each other for several moments. finally, one of them turned to me and told me that they would "gas up the inflatable" and begin searching for my family. ten minutes later, as night fell on the peconic bay, we pulled out of the new suffolk coast guard station. for the next 45 minutes to an hour, we putt-putted around the bay looking for this "mysterious" island on which my family was marooned. one of the coast guardsman stood on the bow with a large flashlight sweeping the beam back and forth across the black waters.

finally, i heard him say, "is that them?" i looked up and saw ellen and nancy waving frantically at the approaching inflatable. they looked upon my bloody body with horror. as we loaded them into the now overcrowded inflatable, they pelted me with questions regarding the circumstances of the accident. they did not believe the truth. i realized that until they were reunited with their loved ones, no amount of reassurance by me would satisfy them.

we drove like hell to greenport and entered the hospital. we found out that fred was in the o.r., having an artery in his head repaired. it had been severed in the accident. mike, happily, had been x-rayed already and the x-rays were all negative. we thanked god no one was more seriously injured and then went back to our motel. it was very late.

the next day, we drove home on the long island expressway. i remember being very anxious each time a tractor trailer passed us. flashbacks of the accident. i silently resolved to stay off the water and out of boats. no place for a palmer.

deliverance at old forge

eim at the water park in old forge, ny, watching as my beautiful, loving wife is repeatedly assaulted by two local teenage girls.

one of the attractions at the enchanted forest water park (i think that's the name of it) is a pool with inflatable boats in it. the boats can be steered, and are equipped with two powerful super soakers which are connected by hoses to the pool itself, thereby providing these super soakers an unlimited supply of ammunition.

mike and kelly, my sons, were in one boat, and my wife got in her own boat to keep an eye on them while i stayed with maggie in her stroller (actually only maggie was in the stroller. i was not).

at some point, the two got separated and ellen ended up on one end of this enormous pool and mike and kelly on the other. at this point, these two adirondack, "deliverance" type chicks, cruised on over towards ellen and begin spraying her with their water cannons. at first, ellen playfully engaged them and shot back at them, but her lack of familiarity with her weapon resulted in spastic, annoying bursts of water splashing (and apparently angering) the two girls from the north country. this in turn inspired them to attack with renewed vigor. relentlessly, they bombarded my wife.

"girls…, enough!" she yelled as she put her hands in front of her face to ward off their accurate fire. "girls…, please!".

but the two girls would not stop. finally, ellen stopped trying to speak and just sat there getting drenched by these two kids until they grew bored and left.

ellen made her way over to the ladder in the pool and climbed out. saturated, she walked back to me and mags. she was laughing her head off. i handed her a towel. "…can you believe that?", she said, as she dried her hair. i told her i was afraid that i was going to have to rescue her.

we got the boys and talked about ellen's adventure as we drove back to clarke's motel on old forge pond, and, like the song "jingle bells" says… laughing all the way.

moo

eim standing on a low stone wall in bright sunlight with my hands on my hips looking down the blackwater river valley in mallow, county cork, ireland. my beautiful bride is with me and i feel like a million bucks.

in july of 1985, my wife and i honeymooned in ireland and stayed at a manor home called loungville house. one evening, after an exquisite dinner, we took a walk around the grounds. i remember seeing a dead rabbit in the pool. very irish. our stroll took us to a low stone wall which overlooked the black-water river valley. it was about ½ mile up to the other side of the valley. up at that top, on the far side of the valley, a herd of bout 50 cattle serenely chewed their cud. or somebody's cud. it was a bucolic scene. i stepped up onto the wall and there in the warm july sun, i cupped my hands around my mouth and let fly with a deep resonant "mooooooo …"

ever so slowly, and one by one, the cows began to descend the far hill. soon they were all moving down towards the river. now some were running, splashing into the river. soon they were all running. running and mooing. my wife and i were in awe as we watched the stampede and heard and felt the thunder of their hooves. up, up the hill they came straight for us. after 20 minutes or so, each and every cow had assembled in a semi-circle around the spot on the wall where my wife and i stood. quiet returned. they didn't know what to do with us, and we didn't know what to do with them. it was a remarkable day on a remarkable honeymoon.

playin' possum

eim holding an adult possum by the tail at arm's length as it twists, snarls and hisses at me.

we had just finished barbecuing in the backyard at 31 pilgrim. as i sat on the deck reflecting and finishing my beer, i spied something out of the corner of my eye. something was walking along the top of the cyclone fence. it was…a possum!

i had often wondered about possums, in particular, their propensity for "playing possum" when they were threatened. recognizing my opportunity, i sprang out of my chair and ran toward the cyclone fence. the possum saw me coming and dove down between the cyclone and stockade fence. i got to the fence and looked down. there he (she?) was, trying to amble away to safety. i reached down and grabbed the critter by the tail, fully expecting it to go limp and play dead. it did not. as i pulled it up, it kept grabbing the mesh of the cyclone fence with his claws. i finally succeeded in pulling the creature out by the tail, upside down. well, this thing behaved like a possessed tasmanian devil. spitting, snarling and snapping its formidable teeth, it wriggled and spun as it attempted to free itself from my grasp. this possum was not "playing possum". i wisely released it and watched it amble up and over my neighbor's fence. bon chance, opossum.

george f. palmer

swimsuit sucking sea

eim staring down at my naked, youngest son, kelly, as he lies face down in the wet sand screaming for someone to bring him a towel.

we had been swimming at the beach at field 6 at jones beach. the ocean was a little rough, but not brutally so. we were body surfing. at one point, kelly got caught in the tumbling wash of a crumbling wave. he emerged unhurt but uncovered. immediately he pronated himself and placed his right hand over his white and cheeky area. next, he began screaming, "get me a towel!". the atlantic had stripped off his suit!. there was no sign of it.

kelly's screaming had attracted quite a large crowd. everyone was laughing and enjoying his predicament. some were pointing. at last, a good samaritan (not even one of his own family!) came forth with a large beach towel and kelly put it to good use as he scampered back to our blanket wrapped up in the towel. when we joined him, he was still a little embarrassed, but soon saw the humor in the situation. a great moment in a great summer.

fire in northport

eim standing in a smoldering privet hedge. my **new** sneakers have begun to melt and all the hair has been burned off my legs.

one afternoon i took my sons mike and kelly up to northport, ny, to visit our friends, t-bone and jill walsh. they had two boys, matt and kevin, about the same ages as my sons, as the boys settled into a wiffle ball game in the front yard, t-bone and i settled into a six pack in the backyard. we sat around a small campfire joking around and telling lies as we sipped our beverages.

at some point in the afternoon, i caught a glimpse of a riderless bicycle fly across t-bone's driveway and on into his neighbor's yard. "..that's a curious thing", i thought. a few seconds later, i saw my oldest boy, mike, running up t-bone's driveway. we made eye contact and mike, as if to allay my fears, slowed to a fast walk and gave me a tentative wave as he walked into t-bone's house. i was becoming suspicious. seconds later, mike reappeared, exiting the house carrying a large plastic cup filled with water. he carried it carefully and swiftly at arms length until he thought he was out of sight at which point he began to run. uh oh…!

alarmed, i walked out into the front yard where i immediately was met by my younger son, kelly. he was frantic. "dad…. mike threw a smoke bomb in the mean lady's yard, and now the whole yard is on fire!". indeed, i now became aware of the smell of smoke. i jumped into my minivan and sped back up

george f. palmer

t-bone's block in the direction from which kelly had come. as i drove down the block i could see smoke coming from someone's yard, perhaps a dozen houses down from t-bone's.

as i pulled up i could see that a row of arborvitaes was on fire. there were dry leaves and brush at the base of the arborvitaes which served to feed and spread the fire. there was also a chicken-wire fence which separated the bushes from the sidewalk, and it was this fence i hopped over in my attempt to put out this burgeoning brush fire.

upon landing amidst the fire, i immediately began stomping out the flames which were by this point rising up above the level of my waist. since i was wearing shorts and sneakers (no socks), all the hair on my legs got singed off and my sneakers melted a bit. quite the adrenaline rush. within five minutes i had managed to reduce the fire to embers and ash.

i suddenly found myself alone, somewhat in shock, and perturbed in the extreme. plus, i was afraid the homeowner might make an appearance any minute. i was debating which way was the easiest way to climb back over the flimsy, chicken-wire fence when i spied young kevin walsh out of the corner of my eye. he was pedaling up the street furiously, and he was carrying a cup in his right hand. he pulled up opposite me and parked his bike. he slowly walked up to the fence and realized that the fire was out. for a moment, there in the smoke and smolderings, we just stared at one another silently. then he threw the water in the cup onto my shorts, got on his bike, and rode away.

good riddance

eim standing in a horse stall on a horse farm somewhere north of leroy, new york. through the barred window i watch the horses i am supposed to be taking care of, trotting off down the road...

sometime in the spring of 1973 (or was it 1974?) the band i was in broke up. i had quit school at brockport state to join the band, wyatt. now with the band broken up and me still being responsible for my portion of the monthly rent, i needed a job. i perused the local papers' "help wanted" sections to no avail. zippo. there was nothing out there. then one day i saw a postcard tacked onto a bulletin board in the local grocery store which stated that someone was willing to pay $2.00 an hour to someone who was good around horses and didn't mind mucking out the horse stalls. not having any other options, i called the number on the card.

it turned out that the horse farm was about nine miles from where i lived in brockport and i had no car. not only that, but it tuned out that the horse stalls i was supposed to "muck out" had not been cleaned in seven months. seven months! i took the job and the guy gave me directions and told me to be there at 8:00 monday morning.

i forget how long the bicycle commute was, but i do remember arriving (late) at the horse farm on that first monday morning. the actual bike ride was, in and of itself, a travail of some magnitude. by the time i got there, i felt as if i had already done a days work. plus, it was hot. the stable consisted of two rows of 10 stalls. one on the right and one on the left. all but two were occupied. it was dark and dank and damp, the only illumination bleeding through the small barred windows each stall had.

the owner explained the parameters of the job and what would be expected of me. upon arriving at the job, i was to let the horses out into the corral one by one until all eighteen were out of the stable. he explained the importance of making sure that the corral gate was locked before letting the horses out. when the horses were out in the corral, i was to commence with the "mucking out" portion of my job. and what a muck!

as i said before, these stalls had not been cleaned in seven months. they should have been cleaned out on a daily basis. it is amazing the prodigious amount of feces and urine a full grown horse can create in seven months. now, multiply that by 18 horses and you will have some idea of the scope and scale of the task which lay ahead of me. augean. the floor of each stall was 3–4 feet beneath the seven month old mélange of stool, urine and matted hay which had been mashed and woven into a ghastly malodorous fabric. one other thing i have neglected to point out is that the barn was infested with horseflies and yellow jackets. lastly, i had to suffer the ignominy of having the owner's overweight 15 year old son, bradley, act as overseer to insure that i did a good job. he did this job with great relish! i hated him. he would always say things like:

"you sure do take a lot of breaks…." and….

"my dad wanted me to do this for $2.00 an hour and i flat out told him no…"

he was obviously very fond of candy apples because he always seemed to be nibbling at one on a stick. there was also a coke machine in the stable. there were slots for coke, pepsi, mountain dew, orange, sprite, and grape. all the slots were empty except the grape. so i would "muck" my day away watching doughboy bradley nibbling his candy apple and swigging grape soda, while offering free advice about the proper technique for pitch forking horseshit, urine and matted straw. you can only imagine how popular bradley's candy apple and grape soda were with the yellow jackets. it was my only joy.

anyway, after stalling as long as i could, i eventually grabbed the pitchfork and stepped gingerly into the first stall. the walls were wet with mildew and incipient rot. hornets and horse files seemed to be involved in an endless series of dog-fights throughout the stall. i shoved the pitchfork into the straw and then stepped on it with my right foot, shoving it deeper into the hay. as i began to use my upper body to get the hay to yield, i realized that this was going to take much more muscle than i had originally thought. redoubling my efforts, i eventu-ally succeeded in lifting a forkful of dung and urine soaked hay into the air and immediately wished i had not. the inde-scribable waft of urine jumped up and hit me like a concrete sledgehammer. i was afraid i might spontaneously combust. i could not breathe. i dropped the pitchfork.

as i hovered in the corner trying to regroup and catch my breath, i noticed a curious thing. the yellow jackets were going crazy from the smell of the newly exposed hay! this, i real-ized, did not bode well for me. i was sweating and ready to puke. i looked over at bradley who was now smiling as he ate that stupid apple. i stuck the pitchfork in again with decidedly similar results. more wafting urine smell, me almost fainting, and a fresh resurgence of frenzied yellow jackets. egad!

at this point i needed to show bradley that i was neither afraid nor defeated. i took fork in hand and began to clean that fucking stall with focus and purpose. i would take a deep breath (don't ask) and mightily wrestle four or five forkfuls of shit-piss hay into the rickety (and i do mean rickety) wheel barrow. i would then wheel it out back behind the barn where a 10' pile of like ingredients awaited me. after unloading the wheel barrow, i went back into the stable for more fun.

again, under the watchful eye of bradley, i attacked the first stall. again, the first forkful, wafting up like straight ammonia, nearly knocked me over. a miasma formed over the contents of the first stall. i worked feverishly at my task (mostly to get away from the yellow jackets), but after hours of backbreaking sweaty smelly toil, it appeared that i had little to show for it. by noon, i had succeeded in cleaning out less than half of the first stall.

bradley announced "lunch, one half hour". he disappeared into the house only to reappear minutes later with a giant hero sandwich. you could see the mayonnaise dripping out the side. i put aside the pitchfork and walked out of the barn and over to where i had lain my bike. i was fuming. i just stood there next to my bicycle staring at the barn. i had no hero sandwich. i had no sandwich at all. i had no money at all. i was starving. and pissed. and i knew that on the other side of that barn wall, bradley was wolfing down that mayonnaise drenched hoagie and washing it down with great lashings of grape soda. farting and burping, too, no doubt. the little fucker.

now i don't know if you've ever found yourself in the following situation. if so, please empathize. as i stood out in the yard, next to my bike, i realized that i was not wearing a watch. how do you figure 30 minutes? no way was i going to go and ask bradley. so i sat there, fuming and very certainly, not eating. the last thing in the world i wanted to do was to go back into that barn and resume my work. to do so even one minute early was unimaginable. so i sat, waiting for bradley to come and tell me that lunch was over and it was time to get back to work.

bradley appeared at the barn door as if he had been reading my mind. "half-hour", he hollered. pavlovian, i followed him back into the barn. he told me that he had to get something from a neighbor's house and that he would be back in less than a half hour. at this point, for some reason i decided to move my bike from behind the barn around to the front. this necessitated me opening the corral gate to cut round. apparently, i neglected to close the gate behind me because twenty minutes later as i was shoveling yellow jacket infested shit, i glanced out the barred window of the stall i was in to gaze upon the spectacle of eighteen horses excitedly giggling as they trotted on down the public side street courtesy of the gate i had left open.

i didn't even curse. they were so far gone already; all i could do was watch as one watches an inevitable car wreck. and then they were gone. i was alone. i dropped the pitchfork and walked out of the barn. i peed against the side of the barn, got on my bike, and began pedaling back to brockport. there was nothing else to do, as far as i was concerned.

as i rode back, i saw the scattered horses in small groups on neighborhood lawns. i had had it. it was irresponsible, but i remember thinking, "…fuck that shit!", and not feeling bad about it one bit.

eim 17

the freshwater lake at caumsett st. park

the rented r.v. in northern maine

me and el during my "fat elvis" period in maine

now you know why i ran away from my first grade class

my uncased guitar atop ellen's v.w. bug

spot,the wonder dog, in front of tent (with poles)

at aspen's pub (with herb) in wantagh

the cows of longueville house

the cows of longueville house

never in a million years

george gets his conch

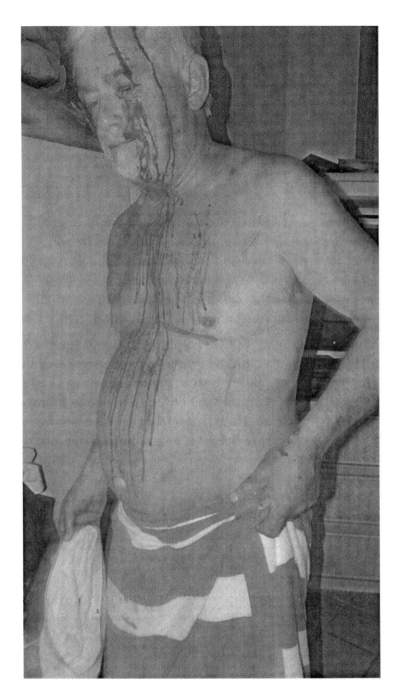

welcome to st. john's

death birth

eim in saranac lake at a campground i cannot recall. it is perhaps 1979 or 1980. my girlfriend and i were about to go camping and were driving around looking for our campsite, #22, if i recall correctly. we were in her yellow vw beetle. as we drove, i noticed a snake slither across the road. i suddenly realized that we had run the snake over. i got out to check it out.

pinned underneath the left front tire and half squished was a female garter snake. she had been gravid and now a dozen squirmy-wormy premature garter snake babies worked their way across the dirt road into the cover of roadside bramble. it was amazing. in death, i was witnessing life. the mother's last earthly act was bringing the next generation to the fore. i was thinking about it for weeks.

elton john

eim sitting on the toilet in the bathroom of an irish pub in malverne called connolly station. i am doing something that is taboo in my world. don't do number two, if you also work there, too.

somewhere towards the end of my second set, i realize that peristalsis had brought about a situation which required the end of my second set. i had to take a dump. no musician (with the possible exception of jackie martling) wants to take a smelly dump in the tiny men's room of whatever venue he is performing in. bad karma. bad zeitgeist. but sometimes, nature calls. that's show-biz.

i stood at the bar immediately after the set and kept my eyes peeled on the door to the men's room. when i was certain that the bathroom was unoccupied, i slipped in and entered one of the two bathroom stalls. i turned to lock the stall door, but as they too often are, it was broken. duty called. loudly. i dropped trou and sat down upon the throne with pants around ankles. i was able to hook my right foot on the bottom of the stall door to keep it shut. it was an awkward position, half sitting/half lying down with my right foot outstretched, yet i sallied forth. all was going well until i suffered a cramp in the plantar surface of my outstretched right foot. a major "ow" was growing there. i had to work fast. i tried to hurry my b.m. valsalva, george, valsalva!

then as if things couldn't get worse, i recognized the voices of two friends entering the bathroom. they entered the men's room and occupied the two urinals which were next to the stall i occupied. my aggressive strained valsalva resulted in not the "one small last plop into the bowl for man ", but rather a long, sustained yet somewhat musical, malodorous fart.

the resonance, timbre and odor of my flatulence caused my friends at the urinals to remark aloud. if i recall their exact words were..."dude, what the fuck"? they chortled despairingly. they were, at this point unaware of the object of their scorn, me.

meanwhile, back in the stall, i mentally debated whether i should talk back to them, thereby exposing my identity or remain silent and hope to leave long enough after them that they hopefully would have moved on and forgotten about their bathroom encounter. yeah right.

it was at about this time that the cramp in my right foot got to the point at which i could no longer hold the stall door closed, and i dropped it to the floor to relieve the pain. of course, as i did so, the stall door swung inexorably open, momentarily exposing me to the rest of the bathroom. i raised pants 'round my ankles to pull the stall door back closed. in that split second, the outer bathroom door also opened as someone walked in, exposing me to the customers who were seated at the bar across from the bathroom. eye contact, however brief, was established. as the outer bathroom door swung shut, i fumbled to retrieve the stall door to shut it. as i did so i turned to my right only to go eyeball to eyeball with my friends from the urinal. "geor-ge" they yelled. "what the fuck..."? i stood there for a moment with my pants around my ankles before silently and slowly pulling the stall door closed. or so i thought. as i shuffled back into the stall, i bent over to pick my pants up, the defective stall door swung back open. i was again exposed. unfortunately for me it was at this point that my two friends from the urinals decided to exit the bathroom. as they opened the bathroom door, i lifted my head and again found myself making eye contact with the people at the bar. again. egad!

george f. palmer

the door swung shut again. i was alone in the bathroom again. i tidied myself up and prepared to exit the bathroom, yet i found myself reluctant to do so. i hate to get laughed at, and i had a feeling that i was about to get it in spades. i was right. as i opened the bathroom a spontaneous and heartfelt standing ovation occurred. i quickly became the focus of the entire bar. "hey... elton john, how ya doin"? "elton john... hey, elton john... i hope everything came out alright..."! everyone was laughing. at me!

there was nothing i could do. in a case like this you gotta go with the flow. i bowed once, crossed to the bar for a beer, and walked back onstage where upon i launched into a fair good version of "broad black brimmer". ah well... that's sho biz!

perception

eim on a portable x-ray run at a large hospital on the south shore of long island. for every pat on the back there's a slap in the face…

somewhere on the third floor, i was explaining to an elderly female patient that i was there to take a portable chest x-ray of her. she said that she understood, and smiled. we made eye contact for a moment and then she said "do you know who you look like?"

"who?", i asked

"michael mcdonald!"

"michael mcdonald. yes. from the doobie brothers, right? white hair, goatee…"

"michael mcdonald", she said again. before i could respond, the curtain which separated the two hospital beds in the room flew open. i was confronted by a tall hispanic woman. her countenance was stern. she slowly looked me up and down and then scowled, "hmmmmm….i think he looks more like… old mcdonald!"

george f. palmer

a clockwork catskill

eim having a good day bein' a bad boy. i guess i was embracing my devil side. my friend and i had gone for a sunday drive in the catskills. the year was 1976. the bicentennial.

back in the day, it was not unthought-of to drive around with beer in your car. we did not understand this danger, and sadly, the police were far too lenient. at any rate, he and i found ourselves driving the blue highways of those beautiful mountains. it was deep summer and the scenery was flat out goregeous.

at about the time our 6-pack ran out, we spied a general store somewhere in the eastern catskills. we pulled in to buy another 6-pack. while we were waiting, we noticed 3 stacks of "happy birthday" hats. the hats were conical and each had a rubber band stapled to it to act as a chin strap. you know the type. they were on sale for a mere 49¢ a piece. my mischievous side engaged, and i purchased 24 "happy birthday" hats for about $15.00. the reason for buying them was simple. we had seen so much road kill carnage on the way up, we found it quite remarkable. we were aware that the n.y.d.o.t. was responsible for removing the deer and other road kill from the county highways. we thought how funny it would be if, when the d.o.t. came around, all the road kill were wearing "happy birthday" hats as if they had been to a party.

with this in mind, we set out on our quest. it was not long before we came upon a deceased, and much mangled, doe on the side of the road. my friend pulled over. i grabbed a hat and jumped out of his car. i ran back to the carcass and knelt down. i lifted the deer's head and slipped the "happy birthday" hat onto her head. disturbing crackling and crunching sounds accompanied my manipulations of the doe's head. i placed the deer's head gently back onto the ground. it was perfect. laughing, we drove on to where we spied a dead, desiccated skunk. again, we pulled over, and again i slipped a "happy birthday" hat onto a dead animal's head. the skunk was so squashed, i had to flatten the hat so that it would stay one the skunk's head. what sport! we continued our drive west stopping for every mangled carcass, to adorn the critters with hats. we did this until we were out of hats. he and i had done such a good job we decided to keep the last two hats for ourselves.

we drove around in our "happy birthday" hats for a while looking for a bit more mischief. it was not long before we found it. our drive took us around one the n.y.s. reservoirs (cannonsville?). we were on a bridge when we noticed a lone fisherman in a rowboat silently angling. we stopped the car.

now you must understand that we had seen kubrick's "a clockwork orange" the previous year and were very impressed. so there we were, overlooking the reservoir, the mountains and the fisherman in the boat. truly bucolic. for a moment.

we peered over the edge of the bridge still wearing our ridiculous "happy birthday" hats. the fisherman looked up at us with marked trepidation. what he made of us, i can only imagine. he offered up a feeble wave, which we returned. we then bent over and picked up some football sized stones from the roadside. we walked back to the side of the bridge and held the heavy stones over our heads. we looked down at the fisherman. the fisherman looked up at us. a summer's moment frozen in time.

the fisherman put his hands up for protection. "boys… don't!", he cried. that was all we needed. we let fly with the boulders. we were not aiming to hit him, just to terrorize him a bit. the boulders splashed around him, kerplunking merrily. in his frenzied attempt to escape us, the fisherman lost an oar and was trying to retrieve it with the other oar. laughing evilly, we, sensing blood, accelerated our attack. we laughed so hard. just to be doing something so thoroughly wrong. exhausted from boulder tossing and chuckles, we jumped back in the car and sped mindlessly and merrily away.

that's how you do this?

eim holding on to the giant penis of a male horse as it ejaculates onto my friends arms and backs.

i spent a lot of the summer of 1973 at gold mill farms, a stud farm up in old westbury, ny. a few of my friends worked there. i knew it was a stud farm, but as i understood it, the "studding" took place privately out in the paddocks or fields or something. i was so wrong.

on this particular day, word passed down to us that they were going to mate two horses in the barn. in the barn? anyway, when the appointed time came, the female horse was led out of her stall and was tethered to a fence by her halter. she was nervous and in estrus. lo and behold, the foreman bellows, "bring me the teaser horse"!

one of the hired hands went over to a distant area of the barn and came back leading a fairly non-descript, older gelding. well… as the gelding approached the mare, someone lifted her tail to give the gelding some nuzzle room access. and nuzzle he did.

the mare's eyes rolled. she shuddered once and let go with an equine orgasm of colossal proportions. it was like a horse pissing on a flat rock. sort of. "get him outta here and bring that colt out here!", bellowed the foreman, "…hurry". two men pulled the teaser horse away from the mare. at about the same time, two other men appeared at the opposite end of the barn with the virgin colt. well, let me tell you…

george f. palmer

the colt got a whiff of the estral wind emanating from the mare and became immediately a possessed creature. he reared up. his eyes flamed and his nostrils flared. he whinnied, and i think whatever he whinnied, it was dirty. all this had a decided effect on the mare, who began an answering whinny. decidedly wanton. she whinnied and reared. and then there it was. this behemoth boner swinging left and right. it was a cross between those bamboo poles that rugs used to be delivered on and the swinging gate on a corral. it was spotted black and pink, like michael jackson. i saw an enormous blood vessel coursing along its side which may have been a second aorta. the tip was bigger than my fist and looked like the end of an egg roll. it was menacing, imposing and intimidating. we were stupeified.

"get him in here, you assholes!", screamed the foreman. then all hell broke loose. two guys grabbed the forelegs of the green colt and literally lifted the front end of the male and set him on top and behind the mare. the mare had another orgasm. this made the colt crazier. the air was filled with pheromones and lust. i was even horny! "guide it in"!, yelled the foreman.

my friend george grabbed the pony's phallus and attempted to penetrate the mare. george, who was a fireman and was used to working with the pneumatic pressures of a fire hose, was completely overmatched by this horse's dong.

i remember thinking that things were reaching fever pitch, and that's when i decided to lend a hand (sorry) for the proceedings. i grabbed hold of this swinging monster and, along with george, attempted to force this battering ram into its intended destination. the colt's legs pumped back and forth. his eyes rolled back until all that was showing was the whites of the great beast's eyes. again the mare whinnied.

and just then, before penetration had occurred, the colt went off. his tally whacker started gushing with such volume and force that we all immediately dropped the thing and ran for our lives. like a 50 pound tube of hair conditioner, this thing sprayed testosterone beestings all over the barn. the foreman took the first blast in the chest and shoulder. it looked like he was melting. my friend george, who was lucky enough to turn around, caught it against his back (although some did go on the back of his hair, too).

and then it was over. the colt, the heavy breathing of the colt as he drifted off to flaccidity, was the only sound heard in the barn. the insemination was a bust. we were crestfallen. so we led the astounded colt back to his stall and the frustrated mare soon followed back to her stall. and i thought as we left the barn; my god... i just jerked off a horse.

soon we were laughing and having some beers. how wonderful and disgusting. oh well. at least i got that goin for me.

less than 10 yards range

eim looking across at the owner of an irish pub in astoria called the (irish pub). he has a small black gun in his hand. he is drunk and he is furious. "gimme back me fookin' fifty dollars!" he has the gun pointed straight at my chest.

it all started out because we had been booked (10 yards range, that is), into the (irish pub), by the owners wife at an agreed upon price. we showed up on the date, put on an excellent four hour show and then began to break down out equipment. we had been well received and the enthusiastic (though loaded) owner had even come on the stage and sang a few "come all yeez" type songs with us.

as herb, my partner and piano player, was breaking down, i approached the bar and requested that the bartender give us out pay. he asked how much we were supposed to get and i told him the price i had agreed to with the owner's wife. no problem. he paid me and i returned to the stage to continue helping herb break down the equipment. the area of astoria in which we were performing was not that great. it was almost exclusively an industrial park. because of this, the parking rules were a little funky. earlier in the evening, i had had to double park my jeep, unload, park several blocks away, and walk back to the (irish pub).

now came the reverse. herb, who had finished breaking down earlier than i, had loaded his equipment into his jeep and was waiting in front of the restaurant for me to return with my car and our pay. i picked up my 1985 jeep and drove back to the (irish pub). as i pulled round the corner, i spied an alarming scene. herb, who appeared to have his hands up over his head, was curbside in front of the restaurant. two menacing figures stood on the sidewalk, the very face of trouble.

as i pulled up, i thought, "now what the fuck is this"? i parked. three pair of eyes bore into me. i had no longer opened the jeep door when the gun toting owner stepped forward and demanded, "gimme back me fookin' fifty dollars". he was 5 yards from me. not even 10 yards range!

i looked at herb. he shrugged, letting me know that it was alright with him if we gave him $50.00 back. "gimmee back me fookin' fifty dollars or i'll shoot you dead!" yeah, yeah, yeah. he had the gun pointed right at me.

"go ahead and shoot… i'm not givin' you back nothin'", i said. i don't know what madness had come over me. i was facing a drunken irish pub owner, who had a gun pointed at me. yet i knew that we had worked and felt that we were in the right.

"if you don't want your wife booking the bands here, then you shouldn't let her. we made a deal, we kept our end, and now you're gonna keep yours!"

"gimme back me fookin' fifty dollars!"

"no, go ahead and shoot"

as soon as i spoke those words, i regretted it. time stood still. somewhere, a dog was barking and all that. all of a sudden, the second man (who i later found out was a cop. he was drunk too), grabbed the owners arm, pulled him back and whispered loudly into his ear. whatever he said to the owner, it worked because he nodded slowly, put the gun back in his pocket and after a parting glare at us, stumbled back into his pub. herb and i just stared at each other for a moment. i suggested driving round the corner to divvy up our pay for i felt it was unwise and unsafe to do so in front of the (irish pub).

we drove around the corner and there, under the light of

a street lamp, we divvied up the 3 – 4 hundred dollars we had made. my hands shook as i counted out the money into herbie's hand. i remember a black and white nypd patrol car cruising past us as we exchanged money in the lamplight. the cops were definitely giving us the hairy eyeball as they slid by.

i became more and more nervous, the more i thought about what had occurred. by the time i got back home in east meadow i had worked myself up into a proper lather. i had just fallen asleep when i was jolted awake by the ringing of my telephone. it was 4:00 a.m.

"is louis there?", a voice asked. "no", i said. "you've got the wrong number." "i don't think so", said the voice. and then… click. he hung up.

as i lay back in bed, i tried in vain to get back to sleep. that wrong number was disconcerting and i kept wondering if it had anything to do with the earlier altercation at the irish pub.

since i couldn't sleep, i grabbed my aluminum baseball bat, went downstairs, put on the t.v. and dozed on and off for an hour or so until i finally got up, showered and went to work.

couldn't in a million years

eim at my sister's house in big indian, new york witnessing a remarkable break of chance.

her yard is about an acre of land and it was into this yard that i brought my sons mike and kelly to practice a bit of archery. i had purchased a bow and a few arrows. so we began shooting and getting the feel of the bow and arrow thing. eventually, it grew into an archery contest. i laid a hula hoop down on the ground perhaps 50 – 60 yards from the boys. the idea of the contest was to shoot your arrow high into the air and have it come down inside the hula hoop ring.

well, the boys had at it with decidedly mixed results. a few arrows flew across lost clove road altogether and landed on the mountainside far away and especially far from the hula hoop. on the 5th or perhaps 6th shot, michael's arrow stuck in the ground maybe 5 – 10 yards from the hula hoop. nice shot! looks like a winner. the preceding shots were all at least 30 – 40 yards from the hula hoop. well, let me tell ya'…

kelly, standing in a different spot from which michael had shot, drew back and let his arrow fly. up… up into the air it soared. it was easy to track against that bluest of catskill skies. the arrow reached its apex and, turning around, began its descent. we watched as it fell to earth.

and then it happened. kelly's arrow came down exactly on top of mike's arrow. exactly. so much so that it bounced off the end of mike's arrow and fell harmlessly sideways a few feet away. omigod! what were the odds? unfathomable.

george f. palmer

the boys laughed and ran to retrieve their arrows, blissfully ignorant of the magnitude of their accomplishment. they could never do that again if they shot everyday for an entire lifetime! i took it in and silently blessed them for their laughter and innocence.

conch and conk

eim about 25 feet under the atlantic ocean and in more ways than one, i am in over my head.

my wife and i had traveled down to key west, florida, on holiday and while there had decided to go snorkeling. neither one of us had ever done it before, but ellen, my girl, seemed to take to it like a… well, you know.

the reef at which we were to snorkel was located approximately 5 miles south of key west. the vessel upon which we rode to the site was a modified catamaran. on each side were benches, each bench accommodating perhaps 18 passengers.

the 5 mile ride out to the reef at which we were to snorkel was choppy and rocky. so was my stomach. so was everyone's stomach. choppy and rocky were the order of the day. and then it began. some asian woman began the ritual heave, replete with gurgling and abdominal spasms. the caribbean 1st mate (or the equivalent thereof,) handed it to tokyo rose who immediately let fly with a foul spew, which was, if nothing else, inspiring to the other passengers. i know this because they began to pass this "puke bucket" around the perimeter of the catamaran. at this point, there were perhaps 20 nauseous passengers between us and the "puke bucket". we watched in horror as almost every passenger contributed his or her breakfast to the "puke bucket". by the time it reached us, it was more than half full. it was heavy and it sloshed and stank as it was handed over.

george f. palmer

someone handed it to ellen, who was somehow able to hand it to me without puking or spilling for which i am eternally grateful. however, once that chum bucket was in my lap, with me staring into the soupy contents, i lost it. i sloppily passed it to the guy on my left as i simultaneously spun my body round so that i could entertain my reverse peristalsis out my fetid mouth over the gunnel and into the sea. it was horrible and the sense of sea sickness stayed with me until we anchored some 10 minutes later at the snorkeling site. so, the fun had not yet begun.

as they anchored the boat, the engines were disengaged and we lay there in the choppy caribbean a rollin' and a rockin' and a rockin' and a rollin'. not the best feeling for post puke passengers. next we had to put up with the first mates pantomime of the proper way to snorkel. had i not been so queasy, i would have enjoyed the comedy. as it was, i wanted to kill him. all i wanted was to jump overboard and give this snorkeling thing a shot. eventually he gave us the okay and into the water we went. my first time. "okay", i thought, "this ain't so bad'. over and over i experimented with the snorkel as i bobbed on the surface. we had ½ hour of snorkeling time before we had to return to the catamaran. the signal to return was to be the 1st mate blowing a whistle.

ellen soon grew tired of my pathetic attempt to somehow remain on the surface for the full ½ hour, pretending to understand the physics of the snorkeling device. she signaled to me (kicked me in the balls with her flipper), and indicated that i should take in a deep breath and dive down with her. "okay…", i thought. "…i'm no pussy!"

and down we dove. and swam. it was beautiful. magical. as i got the hang of it i was overwhelmed by the beauty. two salient points stand out. first, ellen and i were gazing, almost spiritually, at each other as we floated underwater, when, like a herd of buffalo, a large group of barracuda came schooling around a large reef. they were headed right at us. ellen's position in the water was directly in the way of the speeding fish. i'll never forget what they looked like: silver wiffle ball bats with decidedly sardonic grins revealing unbelievably long sharp white needle teeth. i watched as they schooled to avoid hitting ellen. but as i watched, one bumped her under the arm. she was fine, but it reminded me that we were not in our own element, but someone else's. to this day, it was so exciting ellen does not even recall the barracuda bumping into her. we were both overwhelmed. wonderful. five minutes later, the second salient point occurred.

i was really getting into this snorkeling. the more familiar i became with this thing in my mouth, the more adventurous i became (see "midnight cowboy"). at one point i looked down beneath me, and there on the sand seabed was a large, beautiful conch shell! it beckoned. pardon the pun, but though i knew i was in over my head, i dove down. distances can be deceiving in those clear caribbean waters. i got perhaps halfway down when i came to my senses, and thought to myself; "fuck this". i swam back up to the surface. as i bobbed on the surface, enjoying breathing un-snorkeled air, i realized that i was pissed off. i was mad at myself for lacking the moxie to overcome my fears and manly swim the whole way down and recover this wonderful memento. i quickly resolved to give it another shot. gulping the largest amount of air i could, i dove down. back down to where the conch shell (and the threat to my manhood) mocked siren-like to me, egging me onward. i remained focused, swam like hell, got there, grabbed the conch shell, spun upward, swam like hell and hoped to god that i would have enough air to make it back to the surface. my lungs were bursting as i reached the surface (or "breeched", as ellen later described it). but, i had the conch shell! victory!

i began to swim round, looking to show ellen my prize. as i bobbed on the surface, i quickly realized that no other snorkelers were around me. i looked in all directions and saw only water. where's the boat? where's ellen? uh oh! suddenly from behind me, i heard a faint whistle. i turned toward it, and there, about 100 miles away, lay the catamaran. **the mate** whistling away and letting guys like me know how serious they were about keeping to schedule. "omigod". can that really be the boat?

i must tell you that i am not, and never have been, a strong swimmer. luckily, i was wearing a floatation belt that kept me from drowning. it seemed to me that i had perhaps a 75 – 100 yard swim to get to the catamaran. oh boy...

i began to swim. the flippers that i was wearing were very helpful, but my basic lack of swimming skills was rapidly becoming apparent. not only that, but the added awkwardness of carrying this large conch shell added to my dilemma. and so i swam. this is the noise i made as i swam; splash... kerplunk (that's the conch shell)... splish... splash... kerplunk. it was not particularly effective, but it was all i had.

perhaps 15 or 20 minutes later, i realized that i was approaching the catamaran. i had strong doubts as to whether or not i could even make it. yet i swam. when i was perhaps 5 – 10 yards from the ladder that hung from the stern of the cata-maran, i noticed another recalcitrant snorkeler approaching the ladder from the opposite side. we were equidistant from the ladder. i must get there first! and so i swam. splash, ker-plunk, splish, splash, kerplunk, splish, splash, kerplunk... i knifed (sort of) through the waves. i must get there first!

five yards from the ladder, the other swimmer and i eyed each other in a cordial, yet desperate way. it was at this point, i realized that she was a 70 year old woman. at this point in my life i was not yet 40.even steven!

we both got to the ladder at more or less the exact same time. some sort of gender-protocol-victim-prey glance was exchanged between us before i reached out, planted my right hand firmly on top of her head and proceeded to dunk her 70 year old pate underwater as i selfishly scrambled up the ladder, flipper by flipper, into the catamaran.

i sat on the catamaran bench seeking comfort and confir-mation from my wife. as i whined about my travails, the old woman whose head i had dunked climbed into the catamaran. when she and i made eye contact very briefly, i immediately became ashamed. i went quiet. i was quiet the whole way back to key west because i was ashamed. bad george.

george f. palmer

gerry saunders and merle garcia

eim tripping my balls off. it is the first time i have taken lsd. it is not going well. as a matter of fact, it has turned into the worst living nightmare i have ever experienced…

i had one of my front teeth broken off when i played football in the '60's. the dentist put a gold post in and then attached a "permanent crown" to the post. looked good. worked well. no problem. now fast-forward five years. i am in college at suny brockport. i am newly available on the market, having recently broken up with my girlfriend of 8 years. there was a beautiful girl with a smokin' body that lived in brock manor, the dog friendly apartment complex in which i also lived. we flirted. sparks flew when we flirted. unfortunately, nothing ever became of it. that is until one day…

i was singing with my band, wyatt, at the brock manor pub which was located on the property of the brock manor apartments where myself and my fantasy girl both lived. she was there and i sang my little heart out to impress her. after the gig, i spoke to her, and after some shucking and jiving, she told me that she was going to see gerry garcia and merle saunders at the rochester war memorial in two weeks. she then asked if i would like to go with her. would i like to go with her? it was a fantasy come true. "yes…" i said …"i would love to go. i love gerry saunders and merle garcia." the truth is, i knew precious little about the grateful dead and had never heard of merle saunders.

i think some background information here may serve to

help the reader understand how and why the evening became so memorable.

you must remember that this was the early '70's. everyone had long hair, smoked pot, and knew everything about all the cool bands. everyone except me. i still had my football haircut from 1968 and, as a matter of fact, i proudly paraded about campus sporting my "jets 21" football jersey. i was a walking, talking culture clash. so there we were. i had smoked pot a few times, but that was it. in cool circles, i was ever the odd duck. long haired hippies would pass me the bong, but only after having been assured that despite my nerdy and straight demeanor, i was cool. thus it was.

the night of the concert arrived. we (me... gayle... and 3 other deadheads) left brock manor and drove to the great city of rochester, new york. along the way several joints were passed. i was proud to partake and was proud of myself for passing myself off as cool. i fit in. more than that, i figured that i was scoring points with gayle by being so cool and that she would probably be unable to help herself from having wild monkey sex with me at some point after the concert. this despite that fact that i had a dick butkus haircut and was wearing my east meadow high school football jersey with a large "21" on it. nerd/chic, i called it. remember, her other 3 friends had really long hair down to their asses. i stood out. big time.

we arrived at the rochester war memorial and parked the car. as we approached the building, i realized that i had become separated from my peers due to my anxious speed walking. when i finally realized that i had separated myself from my company, i turned round to see gayle et. al. waiting by the car. i walked back to them as i approached them, gayle stepped forward and spoke to me privately. "do you wanna trip?" she asked. as she said this, she held out a stamp sized piece of paper with the jack of clubs (from a deck of cards) sign on it. i looked at her. she looked beautiful. she was wearing a blue "keep on truckin'" tee shirt. it was tight. very tight. she was obviously not wearing a bra. and evidently she was excited about seeing the concert.

"okey dokey", i said, and not having the foggiest idea of what i was in for, swallowed the stamp sized, club faced, lsd. well, let me tell you...

the five of us walked into the war memorial bonded by the anticipation of whatever was to transpire that evening. giggling, we found our seats and settled in to enjoy the music.

i must digress for a moment. you need to understand that prior to my date with gayle, i took a shower (naturally). not naturally, after shaving, i applied liberal doses of <u>english leather</u> after shave to not only my face, but to my nether regions as well. i was speculating that the evening might take an oral turn at some point and i wanted to be prepared.

only moments after applying the <u>english leather</u> to my twig and berries, as the brits say, the entire area exploded in burning pain. plus, the hot shower had opened up all the pores so the alcohol based after-shave really had an opportunity to seep in. ow. really. ow.

anyway, i only mention it because i fixated on it during the concert, due to the effect of the acid. throughout the concert i was aware that my lap was hot, and not at all pleasant, and there was this residual burning.

anyway, back to the show. i do not remember an opening act. what i do remember is flirting with, and ogling, gayle. we looked into each other's eyes knowingly, although what we were knowing still escapes me. anyway, lust was in the air and i was breathing deeply.

the band came on just as the acid began to kick in. they were in fact quite fabulous. spacy. just what i needed. the acid began to wash over me. the music intensified. i was into it. i could not believe the twists and turns their beautiful jazz-fueled riffs took. i loved it, although at one point i remember worrying that merle saunders was pissed off at me and was giving me dirty looks. go figure.

each time a new wave washed over me, i turned to gayle who was also obviously awash in her own glowing buzz. i remember looking into her eyes, deep into the trip, and understanding the sexual connection we were having despite the fact that we had never even kissed and were surrounded by thousands of stoned deadheads. we were turned on and tuned in. the trip intensified. the music was growing louder and wilder. for some unknown reason, i took this opportunity to inform gayle that i thought paul mccartney was a better singer than gerry garcia. oops. buzz kill. she looked at me incredulously as a judgmental scowl slowly spread across her sexy face. oops… my bad. i turned away from her, aware that my *faux pas* could easily put the kibosh on any potential hanky-panky. i sensed the worm turning. i grew apprehensive and began to stare straight ahead and grind my teeth. hard.

i remember staring hard at gerry garcia and then turning to my left where gayle sat, and staring at her as if to say "…hey, whaddya think of that??!!".. no words were being spoken. eye contact, trip contact, that was it. all the while i kept grinding my teeth and growing more paranoid. i began to not like this acid.

i say this because, all the while i was trying not to lose it. tripping and grinding my teeth. that's all i could do. as i sat there in my fearful, paranoid misery, i suddenly felt the post in my front tooth snap and i watched the cap tumble onto my english leather scented lap. uh oh.

try as i might, i was unable to comprehend how this situation had occurred. i looked at the cap in my hand while simultaneously poking my tongue through the gaping hole in my smile. imagine, if you will, my dilemma. i was desperately trying to impress gayle. i was tripping my balls off and i had knocked my own front tooth out. i was embarrassed and scared. for a while i just kept looking down at the cap in my hand and snaking my tongue through my smile.

what to do? the music became irrelevant to me as i focused

on my next move. how do i tell gayle? out of the corner of my eye, i saw her groovin' and dancing to the trippy tunes.

i now began to taste blood because the sharp edge of the snapped post lacerated my tongue every time i darted it through the gap. oy vey.

finally, i could no longer stand it and turned to gayle to explain my dilemma. i nudged her arm to get her attention. she turned her face toward mine. the poor thing. the expression on her face was an exquisite *mélange* of shock, horror and confusion. yet she could not look away. our faces were mere inches apart. i could only stare deeply into her eyes and dart my bleeding tongue thru the gap in my smile. finally she spoke. "stop doing that"., she said. stop doing that? how? i was unable to "..stop doing that." i tried. lord knows i tried, but like a snake i kept sticking my bloody tongue out. plus, i was unable to speak. gayle put her hands over her face to escape my ridiculous visage.

all pretense of me having an enjoyable "trip" disappeared and was replaced by the mother of all nightmares as i sat there wallowing in confusion and trepidation. try as i might, i could not wrap what was left of my mind around what was happening to me. and why did it feel as if my lap were on fire?

completely overwhelmed, i slunk down in my seat and stared only at my lap, still snaking my bloody tongue thru the hole in my smile, and enduring the remainder of the concert. it was an unsexy, unpleasant, and unbelievably long ride back to brockport. english leather indeed.

vacation of a lifetime

eim naked and bleeding, cajoling and pleading, as my children and i slowly circle the cracked-out gunman who repeatedly points his .45 at our skulls.

on june 1st, 2011, my wife and i took our three children, micheal 23, kelly 20, and our daughter, maggie 18, to st johns in the u.s.v.i. for an overdue and well-deserved vacation in paradise. my beautiful wife, ellen, and i had rented a "luxury villa" overlooking the town of cruz bay and the turquoise caribbean. we spent the first two days of our vacation at trunk and cinnamon beaches. gamboling like spring colts or lambs. we were approaching giddy after our two days of sun, laughter and dinners graced by bacchus himself. paradise. st. john's is so beautiful.

we drove our rented jeep back to our secluded villa after dinner on friday night. once in the villa, we frolicked poolside. we luxuriated in the bougainvilla trellised hot tub and played card games until around midnight, when exhausted, we all went to bed.

sometime between 4:00 a.m. and 4:30 a.m. i was awakened by the sound of my wife's voice fearfully, tremulously, horribly screaming "hey…get outta here…" and then… "…don't shoot! don't shoot?" the tone of ellen's voice informed my just waking mind that we were in crisis mode.

i scrambled out of bed and launched myself at the gunman who had opened our bedroom patio door and was attempting

george f. palmer

to push past my petrified, yet still unyieldingly defiant, wife. i caught a brief glance of his concealed face just prior to our collision. he had a doo-rag on and his mouth and nose were covered by a black shirt covering his mouth and nose.

i tackled him. it was so dark. he was so dark. we went to the ground momentarily. we were wedged between the stair rail and the patio table. i was reaching for his throat and he was attempting to pistol whip me but because we were so wedged in, i could not reach his throat and he could not pistol whip or shoot me. he could only softly tap the back of my neck and shoulders with the butt of the .45. then, he was able to push me off him with his right leg. not far, but enough. i regained my balance and went at him again. my thought was to try and drive him off the patio and into the pool, although being a poor swimmer, i don't know what advantage i hoped to achieve with this strategy. moot point. as i dove at him a second time, and unseen by me, he had raised his right hand and pistol whipped me right on top of the old coconut. i went down like a ton of bricks. i saw stars and saw birdies. too apprehensive to pass out, i sprang to my feet. again, i was face to face with my assailant, but this time he had the business end of the .45 pointed at my bloody forehead. the worm, such as it was, had turned. he stuck the muzzle of the gun into my eye. hard. "you wanna see your family die?", he queried. i was reminded of the old jack benny bit.

at this point, my three kids appeared on the patio. my oldest son, mike, immediately ascertained the situation and began to run at the gunman who turned round quickly and now pointed the .45 directly between mike's eyes. "...gimme the fuckin' money", he said as he stepped into mike's face. mike explained, calmly for him, that he was wearing a bathing suit. no money. "...nowadays we use atm cards. that's how it is."

while all this was going on, my saavy wife had slipped back into our bedroom and, unseen by the gunman, dialed 911. as the terrorism on the patio unfolded, my wife was dealing with a u.s.v.i. police operator with a thick accent. my wife could not understand her, and she could not understand my whispering wife. she hung up and now stepped back onto the patio with her hands over her head.

with our hands over our heads we circled the gunman trying to calm him down and talk him down. in turn, the gunman kept pointing the gun at us each in turn all the while mumbling "...gimmee the money, gimmee the fuckin' money". as this psychotic dance unfolded, i caught a glimpse of my younger son, kelly, who suddenly appeared out of the corner of my eye and he was holding an upside down lamp as a weapon, by his side. i was fearful that he was going to attack the gunman and that if he failed to knock out or kill him with the first blow, that bullets were going to fly.

we all kept circling. the only difference was that when it was my turn to have the .45 gun pointed at my face, he would give ma few raps on the forehead while he demanded, "...gimmee the fuckin' money". after making some disparaging comments about my anatomy (remember, i was nude) and demanding money yet again, he took hold of maggie's arm and began to back away. he had the gun in the small of her back. my sons and i began to close in on him, letting him know that there was no way we were going to let him take her with him as long as we were alive. it didn't take him long to decide. he shoved maggie back to us, turned, and walked out into the caribbean darkness admonishing us not to call anybody or "....i'll be back."

steering the earth

eim eight years old. it is 1960 and i am steering the earth.

at this time, my family lived in east meadow in the elgin homes section. it was a small 3 bedroom, 1 bath ranch. my dad had purchased it thru the g.i. bill. there was a cement patio in the backyard. the yard itself was small but well-tended by my father. my mom and dad had purchased a 4 foot above ground pool to help the palmer children through the summer months. because the pool was in the shade all day, the water in it never really heated up. always, too cold. but it was a pool, i was a kid, it was summer and that was that. i was in that pool at 9:00 a.m.. b-r-r-r-r. i waded around the perimeter of the pool to create a bit of a whirl-pool effect. the flotsam and jetsam, leaves, twigs and both dead and dying bugs, soon began to circle the perimeter of the pool. my job was to attempt to flick the bugs over the side of the pool. i would quickly tire of this game. either that or i would run out of bugs. either way, it signaled the end of swim time. one last dive underwater and then over the side and out. i'd grab a towel, step onto the sun baked slate path until the soles of my feet burned, and then dive into the warm sweet grass of the yard, face down. smell that clover! it was from here i learned to steer the earth.

going from the cold of the pool water into the bright warm sunshine on the lawn was a sensual rush and i reveled in it. i would stretch my arms and legs out as far as i could and lie there face down breathing in the fecund loamy air. eyes closed, i would then dig my fingers and toes into the lawn. soon i would feel myself becoming part of the earth. by tensing all the muscles in my body i could sense an almost imperceptible shift in the rotation of the planet. on occasion, i sensed that i had squeezed too hard, and backed off so as not to cause a catastrophe somewhere in the world. then, after steering the world, i would go in the house, have a peanut butter and jelly sandwich and a glass of milk.

george f. palmer

what a mess

eim singing beautifully, but now eim crying and sobbing out of control…

my wife and i had taken our three children to the adirondacks for a week vacation. we had a nice time and were now driving south on the n.y. state thruway on our way home. it was a long drive and the kids were dozing in the back seat. to pass the time (and amuse myself) i began to sing. the song i chose to sing was "the impossible dream" from man of la mancha. on this particular day, i realized that my voice sounded fantastic. such timbre and resonance! as i sang, i put a lot of passion and emotion into it. when i got to the part where the lyrics go "…to be willing to march into hell – for a heavenly cause…", well i just lost it. emeshed in and awestruck by the haunting beauty of the lyrics, and flabbergasted by the mellifluous tones emanating from my throat, i burst into tears. it was all too beautiful. i was overwhelmed.

my wife stared at me. "what is wrong with you?" she queried. through tears and snot, i mumbled "i don't know". my wife began to laugh, which in turn made me laugh. which in turn awakened the kids who in turn also began to laugh and cry. soon were all laughing at me. after ten minutes or so, the kids were back asleep and soon after that my wife dozed off. i was quiet as a church mouse. i rolled south in silence as if nothing had happened. vain silly boy.

t-bone's t-bird's timing chain

eim experiencing both horror and hilarity as i hear a booming backfire from my friends t-bird. the backfire is followed immediately by a large orange fireball which shoots out the exhaust pipe. this in turn is followed by an enormous cloud of thick sooty smoke…

sometime in the early eighties, i received a phone call from my friend t-bone. he told that his car had broken down out by kennedy airport the previous night, and inquired about the possibility of my assisting him in the retrieval of his car. i told him that it would be my pleasure to help, so we piled into my tiny pontiac t-1000 and wound our way over to kennedy.

t-bone explained that his timing chain was broken. i had no idea what a timing chain was. "what do you want me to do?", i asked. he explained that he wanted me to maneuver my car so i was behind him, bumper to bumper. he then wanted me to push him out onto the right lane of the belt parkway. i was to accelerate up to about 40 mph until t-bone stuck his left hand out the window signaling me to back off. at that point he would attempt to start his car. sounded like a plan.

all went as scripted until the point where he signaled me to back off. i backed off and he tried to start the t-bird. well….

four things happened simultaneously. first, the mother of all backfires. really loud. second, a large orange fireball shot out the exhaust. third, a large cloud of dense, sooty smoke escaped from the tailpipe. fourthly, the t-bird shout forward at about 80

george f. palmer

mph, but only for a hundred yards or so. then it stopped com-
pletly and the whole procedure had to be re-enacted.

countless times. tears of laughter wet my face. every time
the t-bird shot forward, i would watch in hilarity as t-bone's
head snapped back. it was like he was astride a rocket. we
finally made it back to east meadow, had a couple of cold ones
and laughed and rehashed the remainder of the afternoon
away. we still talk about it.

"… we're dog friendly…"

eim watching in disdain as my dog, shadow, enjoys a bout of golden diarrhea. we are in a restaurant and the other diners are disgusted and appalled. i too am disgusted and appalled.

one fine summer day my wife and i had gone for a drive out east accompanied by our 5 year old mixed-breed, shadow. after a day of touring, we were driving back west on 25a when we spied an adorable "crab shack" on the south side of 25a. there was a bar with perhaps 10 or so stools and about a dozen tables with umbrellas adjacent to the bar. the floor of the area with the tables was made up of blue fieldstone.

we decided to stop for a bite, so we pulled into the parking lot. we got a prime parking space very close to the tables. it was a beautiful day and we were looking forward to an al fresco nosh. we sat down at our table and noticed that our dog, shadow, had climbed into the driver's seat of our van and was watching us intently through the windshield.

our waitress arrived and seeing us interact with shadow, asked if he was our dog. i told her that he was whereupon she told us that the crab shack was "pet friendly" and that i should feel free to bring shadow to our table. she said that she would bring him a bowl of water, too. *cest manifique!* i went back to the van, leashed the dog, and took him back to our table where i tethered him to my chair. true to her word, our waitress promptly arrived with a bowl of water for our thirsty canine. it was a beautiful moment. idyllic, almost. and then…

george f. palmer

we had each eaten about half of the hamburgers we had ordered when i became aware that the vibe in the restaurant was changing. hushed sounds of disgust began bouncing off the umbrellas, followed by a distinct "...oh...my...god...". i turned round to determine the source of my fellow diners' disdain and was mortified to see that my dog, shadow, had assumed the position and was depositing the contents of his bowels amongst the bluestone chunks. not only that, but his bowel movement was golden diarrhea and it seeped and oozed through the bluestone. several couples left. what to do? the damage had been done. our waitress was nowhere in sight.

red-faced, i bent down, and began to wash each piece of bluestone in the aluminum water bowl, using my napkin as a washcloth. it soon became very disgusting. i say this because the other diners began to exit en masse. the water in the bowl turned brown and my napkin disintegrated in my hand. not good.

my wife went inside to pay the check while i untied shadow from my chair and put him in the van. my wife got back in and we drove off, laughing all the way. not really.

eim...   99

love anger guilt tears

eim late for work. the traffic on hempstead turnpike in east meadow is bumper to bumper passing eisenhower park. the january weather is a foul sleet, two mushy inches of which has already accumulated on the street. i am crying tears of love and shame....

i was driving in an anxious state because i was supposed to be in the o.r. at the hospital i worked in for an early case. now the traffic and weather have conspired to put me squarely behind the eight ball.

as i sat there behind the wheel fuming and stewing, i noticed a woman two cars ahead of me get out of her car, leave the car door open and walk around to the rear of her car to open her trunk. "what the fuck…?", thought i. the light turned green and the woman was still fumbling around in her trunk. i couldn't believe it. i swore at her and honked my horn. leaned on it.

i then watched as she pulled a wool blanket from the trunk of her car and then step-toed through the slush to the sidewalk where a homeless woman was trying to navigate her treasure filled shopping cart through the slush. the sleet was increasing in intensity. as i watched the driver of the car gently place the blanket over the homeless woman's' shoulders, my eyes began to well up in shame for my cursing and horn honking but also the love for this anonymous woman's kindness.

i watched as she dodged traffic, shut her trunk, got back in her car and drove away. my reaction to her compassion was to sob and weep all the way to southern state parkway. i gotta try and be more like that. asshole.

up gore mountain on my face

eim being pulled up gore mountain on my face and stomach. my arms are outstretched and my hands are holding onto the foot rungs of the t-bar that was supposed to gently guide me to the top of the ski slope. i have bent my knees in order to avoid getting my skis caught up. snow is getting shoved down my front as i bump bump bump up the freezing slope…

i am not a skier. never was, never will be. i don't like it. the probable reason for me not liking it is the fact that i don't do it well. i don't like anything i don't do well. i know personally this means that there must be an awful lot of things i do not like. in 1979, back when my wife and i were just sparking, she took me on a ski tour to gore mountain in the adirondacks. the itinerary took us first to gore mountain to ski for a day, and then north to whiteface mountain just outside lake placid for a second day on the slopes. well…

after renting our ski equipment at gore, we made our way over to the line for the t-bar that would take us up to the top where ellen would show me the rudimentary skills needed to "baby-ski" down the run. i had never seen a t-bar no less used one, but i was intrepid. ish. the line to the t-bar was outfitted with ropes on both the right and left sides. the ropes served to help new skiers (me) maneuver their way to the actual t-bar. in theory, a good idea.

getting on the t-bar was a bit tricky. timing was critical. the t-bars ran on a loop continuously up to the top. at the top, the skiers gently skied off. the empty t-bars came back down and hesitated at the bottom for a moment as the new skiers positioned themselves to be whisked up the mountain.

soon it was our turn. ellen skied over to the t-bar and positioned herself perfectly. she then turned her head and beckoned me to join her. i tried. lord knows i tried. the problem was that i was moving my skis back and forth but i was not moving forward. the skis just went back and forth. spinning my wheels. "...c'mon ...hurry...!" cried ellen, who was attempting to linger as long as she possibly could by the t-bar. suddenly, hands reached out of nowhere and shoved me in the direction of the t-bar. i began to move. down, down i went. i think i'm gonna make it! i did! i stood up next to ellen just as the t-bar arrived. success! almost. i had spent so much energy getting to the t-bar that i was huffing puffing and sweating by the time i got there. perhaps this is the reason i chose to sit down on the t-bar. i was unaware that you should never sit down on the t-bar. bad things can happen if you sit down on the t-bar. to wit...

several things happened at once when i sat down. ellen and i sank all the way to the snowy ground, simultaneously bouncing backward and backflipping beautifully off the t-bar and onto the snow face down. both of us. at that moment, i looked up and saw our now unoccupied t-bar swinging back toward us. i reached out and grabbed a rung with my left hand. it began to pull me up the slope. i grabbed hold of it with my right hand, too. also, i should mention that when ellen and i sank down to the ground, the people in the t-bar ahead of us went soaring up into the air for a moment until we fell off, at which point they came plummeting back down. they did not fall off. i bent my knees to prevent my skis from dragging and tangling in the snow. i saw no sign of ellen.

up the slope i went. the people in the t-bar ahead of me were turned around watching my shenanigans with delight. i could read the thought bubble above their heads. it read, "what an asshole!". i felt cold snow being shoved down my neck and chest past my not-quite-zippered-up-all-the-way ski jacket. i kept my head up as best i could because when i put my head down, my forehead plowed a several inch deep furrow through the snow. couldn't breathe, either. better to keep the head up. yup.

after six or seven minutes (days?) or so, the top of the ski run came into view. a small operator's shack was located there. as i watched, a man came running out of it and looked down the slope at me. as i approached the top, he came over to help me up and out of harm's way. it was a process. i had never been on skis before and was experiencing difficulty just standing up. i told the man that i did not know how to ski. he looked at me incredulously, and then gave me a quick lesson in a type of skiing called "snowplowing". he then went back into his shack leaving me standing alone at the top of the run. i stood there stalling a long while. "snowplow, eh?"…alright …i shoved off. i was snow-plowing very hard. too hard. i had my skis pointed in and was digging in mightily with my toes. i was barely moving, going right down the center of the slope at about two mph. this did not sit well with the more experienced skiers who kept zipping by me. kids, too. each and every one of them had an epithet or hand gesture for me. yet down i snow-plowed. i was sweating profusely for i was using every muscle in my body to maintain the wedge of my ski tips in snowplow position. at one point i became emboldened and tried opening up my ski tips a bit to get a little speed up. uh oh. bad plan. i got a little speed up alright, but i had no idea how to steer or stop. i ended up skiing right across the slope and into the woods on the other side. i went headfirst into a soft, deep snowdrift. holy sonny bono! i couldn't breathe. not only that, but i could not extricate myself because of those goddamned skis. i began to panic. i started rolling my shoulders back and forth , to pat down the snow and form an air pocket allowing me to breathe. next, i was able to poke my head out of the snowdrift and roll over onto my back. it was exhausting work. i lay there like a frozen turtle on it's back. a frozen turtle with ski poles and oh-so-cumbersome skis. i was panting and sweating.

what to do? no doubt about it, the skis had to come off. fifteen challenging minutes later i had succeeded in removing the skis. i sat there looking at the brightly colored skis and i began to wonder how i would fare walking down the ski slope carrying my skis and poles. and you all know how smooth and natural one's gait is walking around in ski boots. i considered removing the ski boots, too, and trying to get down the slope in my socks. that would mean i would be walking down the frozen ski slope in my socks, carrying my skis, my ski poles and my ski boots. hmmmm …

i eschewed thoughts of ski boot removal and made my way into an upright position. i put the ski poles under my left arm and the skis under my right arm, and began to stumble/trundle out toward the ski slope. presently, i was at the edge standing there in my ski boots carrying my *accoutrements*. skiers were whizzing by me and it was getting dark.

with utmost trepidation i stepped out of the woods and onto the ski slope. the surface was so slick! i immediately fell down and began descending the mountain on my back and ass. i was trying to retain control of the skis and poles, but then i suddenly began to spin, too. i was cursed at by other skiers and i was completely out of control. i might just as well yelled "…wheeeeeeeee …"

eventually, the slope began to straighten out as i neared the bottom of the run. i stopped sliding. i stopped spinning. and then i stopped. as i made my way to my feet i saw ellen come running over to me. she helped me up and off the slope and into the lodge. over cocoa, we laughed as we re-hashed our day and then began going over our itinerary for the next day. the tour group (of which we were a part), was to go skiing at whiteface mountain in nearby wilmington, ny. i told ellen that i was not up to it. whiteface schmiteface, i ain't goin'. as an alternative, i suggested that we might just spend a quiet day in beautiful lake placid. do some shopping. have a nice lunch. bond. my beautiful girlfriend told me that it was o.k. with her. she understood. i (silently) thanked her and began to look forward to our private date together. just me and her. intimate. i really liked her and was so looking forward to getting to know her better. little did i know that the next day, our quiet day together, would end up as one the most memorable and uproarious, days of our lifetime. check it out ...

george f. palmer

parasail kidnapping

eim 300' up in the air over mirror lake in lake placid, ny, and i am freezing and seething. i have just watched four men kidnap my girl-friend and there is nothing i can do about it ...

the day after our ski *debacle* on gore mountain, found us at the holiday inn in lake placid. ellen and i stayed behind while the rest of our tour group set off to ski whiteface mountain.

ellen and i spent the morning exploring busy little lake placid. remember, this was 1979, the year before lake placid hosted the winter olympics. so much hustle and bustle. and so many people from different countries. it was wonderful! sometime after noon, we stopped at a lakeside restaurant for lunch. we sat at a table by the window overlooking the lake. it was a beautiful day and the view was great. suddenly, a great sail appeared and went past our window. what was that? we craned our necks to see. what we saw was that the "sail" was actually a colorful parachute. the parachute was attached to a snowmobile by a 300' rope. for nine dollars you could put the parachute on and "parasail" once around lake. it took perhaps twenty minutes to circle the lake. we watched as we ate. it looked like fun. we decided to give it a try.

we left the restaurant and walked out onto frozen mirror lake. there was a small line at the kiosk where you paid to parasail. behind us on that line were four young men. as we waited on line, we (ellen) engaged them in conservation and, as it turned out, they were the canadian bobsled team in town to practice at nearby mt. van hovenberg. they seemed like nice guys. we were still talking when the parasail operator cried "…next…". it was our turn. ellen went first. they strapped the harness on her and placed a safety helmet on her head. the man driving the snowmobile took off. ellen began to run, the parachute filled with air, and *voila…* she was airborne! she looked back down at me, waving and smiling. some twenty minutes later she had completed her lap around the lake and slowly floated down, landing gently and gracefully perhaps ten yards from the spot from which she had taken off. she came back to us (us being the canadian bobsled and me) with a frozen face, but it was the smile that was frozen onto her face told the real story. she loved it !!!! as she was telling us all about it, the attendant hollered "…next! …" my turn. i ran over to him and had the helmet and harness attached to me. "start running…" he yelled to me. so i ran. and then i was up. i turned round to give a "thumbs up" to ellen and what i saw freaked me out.

as i was rising up into the wintery afternoon light, i saw the four canadian bobsledders and my girlfriend headed off the ice. they had her by the elbows and seemed to me to be strong arming her. what the fuck? but then again there was nothing i could do about it because for the next twenty minutes i would be way up in the air and far away. i fumed. i had my arms folded across my chest and all the muscles in my body were flexed for combat as i pictured myself rescuing ellen and beating the crap out of the canadian bobsledders. i couldn't wait to get at them. i was, of course, determined not to enjoy my flight. that would have been bad form. despite the view my vantage point afforded, i could concentrate only on vengeance. boy, was i steaming. i could not believe how long it was taking to circle the lake. the twenty minutes seemed like two hours. finally we turned and headed back towards the starting point at the north end of the lake. i was chomping at the bit to land.

the snowmobile slowed as we approached the landing zone. as it did so, i began to gently descend. i couldn't wait. lemme at 'em. and then, no… it can't be! suddenly, i saw one of the bobsledders run out of the restaurant in which ellen and

george f. palmer

i had just lunched. he ran over to the guy in the kiosk. i saw money exchange hands and then i watched as the bob-sleder ran back into the restaurant. next, i saw the guy from the kiosk run out onto the ice. he stood in the path of the snowmobiler with his right arm raised over his head. he was making small circles in the air, his signal to the snowmobiler that i was to be taken on a second trip around the lake. yikes! the snowmobiler gave the throttle some gas and my greatly anticipated descent turned into a most unwelcome ascent. i couldn't believe it. i kicked my legs impotently and dropped f- bomb after f-bomb onto the quiet valley below. i was pissed off and freezing. i circled the lake with a big frozen puss on. when i finally landed, i ripped the parachute off and made a bee line for that restaurant.

the restaurant was on a small rise just off the lake and had perhaps a ten step staircase leading to the rear entrance of the restaurant. my anger was such that i eschewed the staircase and decided instead to cross the snowy lawn diagonally and access the rear entrance that way. i quickly realized that i had made a mistake. the snow was deep. thigh deep. i struggled immediately. my passion and anger were being sapped with each step. my chest heaved. i was sweating profusely and stumbling. i had to reach forward and catch myself with my right hand. my face, my frozen face, dipped into the snow. i pulled my face out of the snow and turned my head to the left. as i wiped the snow out of my eyes i realized that i was facing the restaurant. there, at the window, people were congregating to look at me. they were staring and pointing and laughing. and then... oh, no, ... it can't be... there were ellen and the canadian bobsled team at the window. they, too, were staring and pointing and laughing. and drinking beer! *o mon dieux!* huffing, puffing and stumbling i trudged on over to the restaurant doors. all the fight had gone out of me.

i opened the door to the restaurant. as i entered, the entire restaurant erupted in applause. i looked like a yeti. i had been up in the frosty freezing air for three quarters of an hour. i was snowy, angry and exhausted. my beautiful girlfriend appeared, walking towards me with an ice cold budweiser. the applause continued. the members of the canadian bobsled appeared from behind ellen. they were laughing and clapping and now clinking glasses with me! i had just been plotting to kill them all! ah, well, the lord moves in mysterious ways. i toasted them.

at any rate, as we partied on into the evening, they invited us to bobsled with them from the top of mount van hovenberg the next morning. we said, "okay", and made plans to meet them at 8:00 am. we met them and we bobsledded down from the top of mt. van hovenberg. we zigged and we zagged. what a rush! but this is a story for another day...

honeymoon hijinks

eim on my honeymoon. not coincidently, eim also nude, drunk and jumping up and down on the bed at the fitzpatrick motor inn over by bunratty castle in ireland. suddenly, car headlights come shining through the unclosed blinds exposing me in all my glory to the occupants of the car. i immediately flattened myself out on the bed but...too late.

it was late june, 1985. while honeymooning in ireland, my wife and i attended a medieval banquet at bunratty castle. the gig was that the tourists were seated around a large oak table and were treated as if they were guests at a great feast. dinner, including mead, (yuk), was served by vuluptuous "wenches" while musicians played lute and lyre tunes as we feasted.

the young couple sitting next to us at the feast were also honeymooning in ireland. turns out, they were also from long island. nassau county somewhere. they were staying at a relative's farm in pallas green, county tipperary. after the bunratty feast, we retired to our motel, the fitzpatrick motor inn, which was next door to the bunratty castle. more beer was consumed. the couple invited us out to the farm for the next day. we agreed. they told us they would be back at 9:00 a.m. to pick up for the ride to tipperary. we said our "goodnights", and as i closed the motel door, i was overcome with elation (and maybe guinness). i was so happy. thrilled.'

i grabbed my wife and danced her 'round for a moment. then i kissed her. she was so beautiful. i was still giggling as i took my clothes off. i went to hold her, but she held her arm outstretched saying, "...no. c'mon its late. i'm tired. let's just go to bed". in my marital bliss, i leapt onto the bed, and nude, began to jump up and down on the mattress. what fun!

suddenly, car headlights came shining in through the unclosed blinds exposing me in all my glory to the occupants of the car. i immediately flattened myself out, but... too late. oh well...

the next morning, the couple we had met at bunratty castle picked us up at the appointed time. my wife and i sat in the back seat of their car for the drive to the farm. i was tired and crapulous. after about 15 minutes of driving, the husband (i can't remember his name) turns round to us and says, "you're not gonna believe this, but last night when we were leaving the motel, we saw this naked guy jumping up and down on the mattress! boing, boing, boing. it was the funniest thing i ever saw!" ah ha ha ha ha.

george f. palmer

epilogue

eim looking back on the words i've just written and realizing that whomever reads these words will formulate an opinion of me. this includes my family. i wrote these stories down to celebrate the warmth and comfort of memories. i did so candidly, perhaps too candidly. these are stories from my life as i remember them – verbal snapshots from a memory bank. candor is a double edged sword; it illuminates, but the things it illuminates can be embarrassing and, as the man said, "...facts are facts, and facts are stubborn things".

i know that these stories by no means tell the complete story of who i am. i also know that because i wrote these words the skewed version of me is out there. or is it skewed? i am comforted that those who know and love me will continue to know and love me.

is it life that is crazy or is it me that is crazy? personally, i think a daily cup of crazy is good for your funnybone. never have more than one cup, though. as for my life, it was what it was and it is what it is. i'm happy where i am now. it has been an interesting road.

i would like to thank, and apologize to, everyone involved in these stories. after all, eim me. and, as omar said...

"...the moving finger writes, and having writ, moves on...

nor all thy piety nor wit shall call it back

nor all thy tears wash out a word of it".

eim...   113

CPSIA information can be obtained
at www.ICGtesting.com
Printed in the USA
LVOW10*1542140517

534490LV00018B/522/P